Translation Theories Explained

Translation Theories Explained is a series designed to respond to the profound plurality of contemporary translation studies. There are many problems to be solved, many possible approaches that can be drawn from neighbouring disciplines, and several strong language-bound traditions plagued by the paradoxical fact that some of the key theoretical texts have yet to be translated.

Recognizing this plurality as both a strength and a potential shortcoming, the series provides a format where different approaches can be compared, their virtues assessed, and mutual blind spots overcome. There will also be scope for introductions to specific areas of translation practice. Students and scholars may thus gain comprehensive awareness of the work being done beyond local or endemic frames.

Most volumes in the series place a general approach within its historical context, giving examples to illustrate the main ideas, summarizing the most significant debates and opening perspectives for future work. The authors have been selected not only because of their command of a particular approach but also in view of their openness to alternatives and their willingness to discuss criticisms. In every respect the emphasis is on explaining the essential points as clearly and as concisely as possible, using numerous examples and providing glossaries of the main technical terms.

The series should prove particularly useful to students dealing with translation theories for the first time, to teachers seeking to stimulate critical reflection, and to scholars looking for a succinct overview of the field's present and future.

Anthony Pym
Series Editor

Cover Design

Rembrant nella sua prima vita artistica

by Giuseppe Moricci
(1806-1879)

Courtesy of Elena Tognini Bonelli, Florence

Translation and Literary Criticism

Translation as Analysis

Marilyn Gaddis Rose

St JEROME
PUBLISHING

Manchester, UK

First published 1997 by

St. Jerome Publishing
2 Maple Road West, Brooklands
Manchester M23 9HH, United Kingdom
Fax +44 161 905 3498

stjerome@compuserve.com
http://www.mcc.ac.uk/stjerome

ISBN 1-900650-04-5
ISSN 1365-0513

Copyright © Marilyn Gaddis Rose 1997

All Rights reserved, including those of translation into foreign languages. No part of this publication may be reproduced, stored in a retrieval system or transmitted in any form or by any means, electronic, mechanical, photocopying, recording or otherwise without either the prior written permission of the Publisher or a licence permitting restricted copying issued by the Copyright Licensing Agency (CLA), 90 Tottenham Court Road, London, W1P 9HE. In North America, registered users may contact the Copyright Clearance Center (CCC): 222 Rosewood Drive, Danvers MA 01923, USA.

Printed and bound in Great Britain by
St. Edmundsbury Press Ltd, Bury St Edmunds, Suffolk

Cover design by Steve Fieldhouse, Oldham, UK (+44 161 620 2263)

Typeset in Cairo by Delta Typesetters
Fax: +20 2 3358990. Email: rusanaa@rusys.EG.net

British Library Cataloguing in Publication Data
A catalogue record for this book is available from the British Library.

Library of Congress Cataloging in Publication Data
A catalogue record of this book is available from the Library of Congress.

Contents

Preface

To Musers ... to Mockers

"Aux rêveurs... Aux railleurs", so reads Villiers de l'Isle-Adam's dedication to *L'Eve future* (1885), his novel about a fictitious Thomas Alva Edison. The above heading is from my translation, which I entitled perhaps a little too unambiguously, *Eve of the Future Eden* (1981).

That translation was published over fifteen years ago. Now the coupling 'dreamers/deriders' immediately comes to mind, but I am glad I did not use it. Euphonically, it may not be much more jarring than 'musers/ mockers', but semantically it summons 'impractical' (from dreamers) and 'derisive' (from deriders) and makes of a dichotomy a unity. That is, Villiers is not so much addressing this astonishingly clairvoyant novel to two types of readers, both the sympathetic and the critical, as to two groups of readers whom he merges as objects of his irony.

But as we live through another *fin-de-siècle*, I would now incline to 'in reverie and raillery'.

First, I am so inclined because the ambivalence in the novel leads me to believe that Villiers included himself in both camps. Not only would his intended audience be comprised of readers who reflect and readers who reject, but his implicit narrator would be engaged in both dreaming and debunking.

Second, since Villiers de l'Isle-Adam is secure as an important minor writer, partly because the definition of French literary 'Decadence' was inferred from his example, perhaps we should try to be as close as possible to his actual words as the two languages permit. In particular, if his eerie fluctuation between ellipsis and redundancy defines Decadent style, then perhaps we should let his French echo through our English.

(Third, as one of the 'Amis de Villiers de l'Isle-Adam', I look back on his star-crossed career with affection and pity.)

All the near-synonymy and alliteration just marshalled demonstrates that even between two languages so historically and culturally intertwined as French and English, there is a great deal of meaning and melody. The enhancement of literary experience by translation comes not only from what the author genially wrote and what the translator felicitously found but also from other words or ways they – or we – might have used instead.

That is what this essay in the *Translation Theories Explained* series sets out to do: to demonstrate by example how the linking of translation studies and literary criticism enriches the reading of literature and other serious pieces of rhetoric throughout the humanities and social sciences. Ultimately I advocate a way of reading literature. This is a 'stereoscopic' strategy that will accommodate whatever mode of translating is being followed from the most literal to the most free.

Such an essay should empower those best qualified to engage in it: translators and teachers of comparative and general literature. Thus, although I hope anyone who deals with texts that have literary pretensions will find something provocative in the pages to follow, this essay is principally addressed to translators, comparatists and their advanced students. In American postsecondary institutions, these faculty will be on the same team, playing interchangeable positions. In such a team some members will teach languages other than English and will often teach in languages other than English. Some members of the team will take turns leading translation workshops or creative writing workshops. However it should be stressed that I have seen the strategies of stereoscopic reading used productively throughout the humanities and social sciences wherever the interpretation of texts is at stake. Literature, after all, can and should be very broadly defined.

Translation and literary criticism, our main terms here, have always been historically interdependent. But over the past quarter century, proponents of both literary criticism and post-Heideggerian philosophy, when classified together as Postmodernists, have found in translation a key to literary theory. Their use of translation, although it stops short of the use to be made of it in the following pages, can be a cue and a justification (if such is needed) for using translation as a critical method both for analyzing literature and teaching it, not to mention translating it. Translating brings us *into* a literary work, in the usual sense of immersion and identification.

In our teaching and research a translation does not only allow access to a literary work that would otherwise be closed. A translation challenges readers with a boundary. But in setting a provisional boundary, it also establishes an interliminal space of sound, allusion and meaning where readers must collaborate, criticize and rewrite, thereby enriching their experience of literature. From this perspective, literature can only gain in translation.

In this connection Villiers' *L'Eve future* is a mirror image of reception

2

and process. Except for the inventions ascribed to him, Villiers' Edison is ahistorical. Nor does the Menlo Park of the novel, a baronial late nineteenth-century manor from the ground floor up and a Rosicrucian temple cum laboratory below, resemble the New Jersey Memorial State Park and Museum devoted to Edison. As translator, I received and returned the novel via English-language dissemination. (By now I have lived with the novel four times as long as the author, who died when he was just past fifty.) Villiers' novel was a Frenchman's allegorical dramatization of inventiveness, but as readers we witness relatively little action and overhear very few dramatic lines exchanged. Rather we listen to alternating monologues that describe, after the fact, what has happened. These monologues are verbal representations in which the words themselves are almost as important as what they represent. Villiers intended the novel for the *rêveurs* and the *railleurs*.

My essay is an American's discussion of translation studies and literary criticism, in which much space is accorded to writers like Villiers and his better remembered sometime contemporaries like Baudelaire, Flaubert, George, Poe, Stendhal and Yeats. Although American, I am a lifelong Francophile and Hibernophile, yet irremediably a Missourian wherever I live, and Missourians begin their lives occupying simultaneously the Midwest, the Border South, and the Show-Me State. In the language of translation, we are used to living amidst disjunctive cognitive mappings.

Hence, this essay will be an American perspective based on an American's reading and an American's experience as a teacher and trainer in the American postsecondary educational system. It is a perspective offered with the hope it can be shared with colleagues elsewhere from whom she has learned so much. Offered in reverie and raillery.

1. Postulates of Literary Criticism

"Congratulations on rediscovering the 1939 interpretation of 'Sailing to Byzantium'." So wrote a senior scholar in 1975 to a doctoral student preparing to defend his dissertation at the State University of New York at Binghamton. As the outside member of the dissertation committee, I shared the candidate's chagrin. Now, decades later, the sarcasm no longer seems the ultimate deflating insult. If not a compliment, it was at least an open acknowledgement of something that exists in literary criticism, and an implicit acknowledgement of a claim of literary knowledge. Obviously, the graduate student, who subsequently became as well-established in Modernist scholarship as his critic, was being told that his Postmodernist critical strategies, new at the time, had revealed nothing new about the Yeats poem. We receive new critical approaches with mixed expectations. They should justify themselves by uncovering new facets of familiar works; but should not such approaches also touch upon, even reinforce, consensus? What the senior critic was also implying, possibly unwittingly, was that there is a stable core of something – call it meaning – in 'Sailing to Byzantium' and, by extension, in literature generally. A literary work, while capable of eliciting ever new reading experiences, still has an irreducible integrity. Its manifestation is a certain ordering of certain words in a certain language.

But beyond those words in that order the literary work has at any moment and with any reader a certain 'aura'. The greater the work, the harder it is to describe that aura, let alone articulate it. We can, however, translate it. We do so by replicating its lexical and syntactical cues. Not that a translation will transfer the aura. Neither completely nor for all time. Have we all not agreed that literary translation is flawed by nature and that poetry translation is almost always a contradiction in terms? Put another way, if a translation is successful, has it not become something else? Yes, yes, yes. But the translation will demarcate the boundary thresholds between the work itself, the translation, and the interliminal space that the translator has enclosed both as proxy author and as proxy reader.

This is true for verbal expression in any genre, at any level of discourse. But since 'Sailing to Byzantium' has been mentioned, let us merely try putting into French the short, simple declarative sentence of the first line: *That is no country for old men.* An interlinear might be *Ce pays-là n'est pas pour les vieux* (back-translation: 'THAT country is not for old men'). Eight syllables in each. It doesn't sound bad, but does it say as much as the English? What ideas are being included between Yeats's line and ours?

First of all, *That* seems to refer to Byzantium, a country long overlaid by strata of history, to which Yeats's imagination turns, fixing on the fifth and sixth centuries. It is not a place where he could go in fact. Living there would be an imaginary situation, and the poet (in his sixties) has discarded it as a viable condition. Thus, perhaps the conditional mode is called for: *Ça ne serait pas le pays pour les vieux* ('That would not be the country for old men'). Of course, *vieux* ('old', masculine plural) could include both men and women, so we are already, almost inadvertently, introducing a feminist reading. Do we want to add *hommes* ('men')? Perhaps not. Yeats may be referring to the fact of ageing generally, but in gendered terms; in which case, we should stay with *vieux* alone or, at most, add *gens* ('people'). On the other hand, if we incline to a biographical reading and know that Yeats in 1928 would have been worried about virility as well as productivity, we might even add *mâles* ('males'). Or, since the next sentence tells about the amorous young, we could go straight to the implications with *Ce pays-là exclut les vieux* ('that country excludes old men') or *Ce pays-là ne reconnaît pas les vieux* ('does not recognize them'). There is also the option of trying to restore the energy missing in all these French approximations but forcefully present in Yeats's opinionated pronouncement; we could use something like *Faites attention, les vieux, en ce pays!* ('Watch out, old men, in this country!)

There is no need to belabour the point further. It is easier to articulate the range of compressed implications we sense in the English sentence if we try to transfer it into French – or any other language.

This process holds true for any literary work. The passage of time and a multitude of readers can bring about changes in how a particular work is perceived and hence interpreted. The work itself appears to change. But doesn't it maintain a sameness, even though it cannot be read the same way? Native readers of the language in which it was written will keep finding something familiar when they return to it. For a much-read poet of high seriousness like Yeats we have a re-reading dilemma within our own language. Should we return to a textbook of one of our first readings where scribbled jottings and coloured pencils remind us of our own repeated re-readings and impose those readings on us? Or should we confront Yeats on a virgin page, trying to read him without such interference?

No marking so definitively dates or individualizes a reading as does a translation. A translation proclaims that this is what the work in question meant to that translator on the date he or she declared the translation finished. It marks an understanding that is time-bound or ideology-cued. Further, if we reflect on matters of taste, rhetoric and talent, we have to recognize that tyrannies of lexicon and prosody may have diverted translators from what they thought the work meant; they may have imposed a reading for us that is still not entirely or spontaneously theirs.

The work is a resilient axis in a circle or a globe with a circumference that wavers and shifts – both horizontally and vertically.

But what that infinitely expanding and contracting circumference contains belongs to the axis and is part of the work's potential, both with its actual contemporaries and those of its future. Translation provides the most clearly demarcated circumferences, rendering visible or visualizable the richer contents enclosed. Now we can hardly insist that readers translate as a general rule. After all, readers read in the language(s) they know, and when they don't, they read a translation. Indeed, our reading habits as bilinguals may even work against literary appreciation enhanced in this way because if we are fluent readers, we do not consciously translate as we read. The point is that if we use the translator as our reader/choragus, as our proxy reader, we force ourselves to articulate our own reading. We sputter, 'But that's not what the word means!' or exclaim, 'That translator does not speak for me!' And then we must say what the word does mean or what we would say if we had been the translator.

If we do not juxtapose a work and the translations it elicits, we risk missing many a gift inside the borders. Each phrase, each sentence, each paragraph has a boundary that is more a threshold than a barrier. Those are the boundaries of the original, the text as first composed and those of its counterparts in translation. Each boundary can be crossed inasmuch as a threshold provides an entry.

In between is the 'interliminal text', unwritten but paraphrasable. This interliminality is the gift translation gives to readers of literature. It is what translation theory, broadly construed as a conceptualization of what translation is and does, contributes to literary criticism. Herein lies the premise of the ensuing essay: Without the reading strategies highlighted and focalized by translation studies, we will miss much of what literature has to offer. Put positively, translation studies points us to a sure way of participating in literature and adding to its richness.

*   *
*

References to the 'between' are not uncommon in anthropology, continental philosophy (the North American designation for the post-Heideggerian speculative tradition), cultural studies, Deconstruction and Postmodernism. Yet I have not encountered 'interliminal' as a noun or adjective used in the way I shall do so in this essay since the day in 1988 when I asked a colleague for the word to designate what lies between the source phrase and the target phrase. I thought there must be a rhetorical term that I either did not know or could not recall, and I needed some word for the application I was going to extrapolate from Jean-François Lyotard's *La Différand*. My colleague, Stephen David Ross of the State University of New York at Binghamton, rejoined 'interliminal'. He never uses it, but I have been using it ever since.

I have illustrations from poetry and prose. Essays and orations would have provided examples, but fewer, and I believe they would be already shared in readers' personal repertories. I have deliberately avoided examples from drama. First, I believe the requirements of the intended audience and the vision of the director make drama translation as much a matter of theatre as of translation studies. Second, this point has been made in several specialized works such as the excellent studies of Shakespearean translations by Annie Brisset and Romy Heylen. Third and most important, my premise is based on reading habits.

*   *
*

This means that I shall not address all the basic questions that arise whenever translation theory is considered. Theories vary by how much of translation they try to account for, or, to put it another way, which facet they put in the key position.

If the emphasis is on practice, the 'theories' look like conceptualized manuals. For example, Mildred Larson's *Meaning-based Translation. A Guide to Cross-Language Equivalence* (1984) is a guide for the beginning practitioner in the field (and is particularly fascinating because of its use of non-Western languages.)

If focused on process, 'theories' follow the steps the mind must take, as inferred either from a comparison of texts or from codified practice deriving from a comparison of an original text and a translation judged to be satisfactory. For example, Eugene A Nida and Charles Tabor's *Theory and Practice of Translation* (1974), with a far more restricted spectrum of examples than Larson's, shows how to segment components of meaning. Both Larson and Nida/Tabor make assumptions about non-Western languages on the basis of Western languages. This is not a criticism, certainly not a charge of colonialism. Western translators have had to proceed from experience with their own language base.

If they emphasize product, 'theories' describe the norms of rhetoric being followed by the translation. For example, Gideon Toury's *Descriptive Translation Studies and Beyond* (1995) argues for successive descriptions through time and concurrent descriptions of the various accepted genres in a society. Although it was not an innovation to propose commenting on the metamorphoses of a literary work through translation over time, like Homer through the ages, Toury and his students have promoted paying attention to the minute detail, focusing on items like prepositions and participles. They have also advised examination of versions accepted in popular culture. For example, one can compare the versions that emerge when popular culture 'translates' a literary classic: consider a close literary translation of Victor Hugo's *Notre-Dame de Paris* ('The Hunchback of Notre Dame') and the Walt Disney Corporation's *Quasimodo*.

If the focus is on the nature or essence of translation, 'theories' place translation metaphorically in the perceived but barely affable world of the mind. Here, of course, I am thinking about Walter Benjamin's canonical essay 'The Task of the Translator' (1923, 1968), to which I shall refer again and again throughout this discussion of translation and literary criticism.

My discussion will concentrate on process and product but with considerable reliance on intuitions on the nature of translation. Throughout I shall emphasize what literature gains in translation.

Although experienced translators must have been trying to explain or justify what they do long before Cicero and Saint Jerome, I give notice that in my idiosyncratic American amalgamation, I date the beginning of modern translation studies with Eugene A. Nida's 1947 essay on translation principles, published by coincidence when machine translation was getting started. I note that Wolfram Wilss (1985:13-14) and Georges Mounin (1976:80) also give Nida's essay preeminence. I consider the next watershed date to be 1975, when George Steiner, in *After Babel*, recuperated Walter Benjamin's essay 'The Task of the Translator' (1923), even though Harry Zohn's clarifying translation had been available for seven years. Scholarship exploded exponentially after that point. The descriptive empirical methods, introduced in 1976 as the polysystem approach (and still being referred to by that label) demonstrated systematic strategies for translation analysis. I do not underestimate their durability in translation theory, nor their usefulness in keeping attention foregrounded on texts. However, for the purpose of the ensuing essay, they have not been as important as the recovery of Benjamin. The recovery was taken into (and over by) literary criticism and, to some extent, has influenced translation practice in the academic press.

Benjamin's own 'afterlife' contributes to the expansive phase that cultural history is now going through, a phase which in its turn validates the interliminal readings this study will promote.

2. The Compatibility of Translation and Literary Criticism

Translation and literary criticism: in this coupling, translation studies leads, follows and supports. Indeed, when we consider that even the most erudite or long-lived critics cannot know all the languages they need, we recognize that literary criticism is dependent on translation, which, in turn, gains from the scrutiny of the latter. In tandem, translation and criticism enhance the understanding and appreciation of literature. For the serious study of literature they should be considered an indispensable combination.

Without translation, obviously, literatures could not be experienced outside their usual areas of language use. Without criticism, nearly as obviously, literatures could not build up the traditions that help preserve and disseminate them. When a literature loses the active users of its first language of expression, it is lost in substance as well, unless translations have survived as records. We can cite Etruscans, Amerindians, innumerable pockets of limited dispersion throughout the world: these are languages that failed to recruit a sturdy literate survivor with a good memory and hence are lost to us. There were, for example, once about 500 languages spoken in North America; only 100 were still spoken in 1995. The total went to 99, on 9 January 1996 when Red Thunder Cloud, the last speaker of Catawba, died, leaving only a few recordings for the Massachusetts Institute of Technology and the Smithsonian Institute.

Classical Greek and Latin literatures survive because of translation. The record of some documents would have been lost had it not been for Arabic translations; the Renaissance in the West revived Latin as a language for serious matters, but hardly for serious literature. Even the teaching of classical languages depends on translating to and from a vernacular, and the teaching is limited: in North America, beyond ecclesiastical circles, studying these languages has become a matter for specialists needing a research tool, as is the case of the Classical language requirement in some – not all – comparative literature doctoral programs. The world languages that displaced Greek and Latin are also the mediators which, through translation, have kept them alive. Today, when we witness a resurgence of linguistic nationalism, we need to remember that in fostering languages of lesser dispersion we must likewise keep their link to world languages such as Arabic, Chinese, English, French, German, Greek, Italian, Japanese, Latin, Russian and Spanish.

Translators and thus translations are mediators. Of course, in their appropriation of something not theirs to begin with they risk damaging or misrepresenting what they have appropriated, even when they are benevolent or unthinking. Mediators may be inherently incapable of complete neutrality. And yet, whether presumptuous or subservient, they are indispensable links. It will be argued here that they not only cross boundaries, they also simultaneously set them and break them. But literary criticism, not cultural imperialism, is the focus here.

In the last chapter we found it was possible to translate a single line from a much anthologized poem by W. B. Yeats, yet we were by no means able to render in one French line all the meanings that seemed to be encapsulated in the English. Indeed, we used that apparent failure to promote the value of translating. Such a 'failure' needs to be reconsidered. It surely advances the cause of neither translation nor creative writing to assert that translators are *poètes manqués* ('would-be poets'), as if creative writing were a completely spontaneous activity and translating an entirely willed activity suitable only for second-rate writers. Poets themselves, of course, must supplement inspiration with industry and perseverance in order to translate a situation or feeling into language. Many translators proceed, at least in part, in an inverse use of industry and perseverance to some kind of re-enactment of the situation that will help recover a feeling akin to the inspiration.

Nor, to move directly to the topic at hand, is the cause of translation and literary criticism advanced by claims that one is superior to the other or that both are superior to creative writing. These assertions are snares set from time to time by critics or theorists trying to goad the complacency of common sense but generally arousing a dismissive response that sends both translation and literary criticism into disregard, if not disrepute. What both translation and literary criticism can be in certain circumstances is a distillation or expansion of the text in question, but neither necessarily results in a finer product or higher mental process – if 'finer' and 'higher' make much sense in such contexts.

Both translation and literary criticism are, as copyright law attests, derivative, deriving from a prior text. A translation can be considered a better piece of writing than the original literary work. When we get to Baudelaire as a translator of Poe, we should keep in the back of our mind that for decades American literature specialists, especially in the United States, have speculated that Baudelaire surely improves Poe. I happen to disagree, but the argument is plausible. Or we can value a critical essay on a work more highly than we value the work, whether the critic was referring to the original or the translation. When we get to Baudelaire in translation, we should keep in mind that Edmund Wilson's *Axel's Castle* and Yeats's introduction to *A Vision* are still studied, but that Villiers de l'Isle-Adam's *Axèl*, the armchair drama referred to in both works, is known chiefly by hearsay, even with translations in print. (Unstageable, it has had fewer than a half a dozen concert readings in over 100 years. Although Yeats was present for a reading on 26 February 1894, he was a monolingual and could not read a translation until the early 1920s.) But first there must be the literary work.

Literary translation is a transfer of distinctive features of a literary work into a language other than that of the work's first composition. But literary translation is also a form of literary criticism. It is just as offensive to assert that translation is the only valid form of criticism (i.e. How can you understand a work if you cannot translate it? i.e. express it in your own words?) as to assert that works can only be understood in their original language (i.e. How can you understand a work if you cannot read it?). Neither snobbery advances the understanding and appreciation of literature.

What translating does is to help us get inside literature. We can do this both as translators, professional or amateur, and as literary critics, provided we make use of translating. We can do this directly, by putting into our own language the literature we are studying, or indirectly, by comparing translations. Either way we should feel we are moving inside what we are reading, examining literature from the inside, a way of making sure that we feel it from within. Either way, in short, provides a mechanism that enforces its own direction and momentum. It is even risky to use translation as a critical tool and/or end in itself if the work to be translated is not one we find congenial.

For works for which we have little or no attraction, it is probably psychologically safer to describe literature from the outside, and if we need to ascertain only the overt ideas or 'information', an outside description is nearly as accurate and complete.

Further, it must be admitted that with works for which we discover an overwhelming affinity, that discovery alone will get us inside. We need not bother with translating or criticizing. For enjoyment we do not need to know we are reading a translation. In fact, in some literary forms, we may not need to know the language; following the drift of language may suffice. Opera and film have fans who ignore supertitles and subtitles. But wouldn't such fans admit that knowing the libretto or the screenplay in their own language adds to their experience?

Surely it does, even when the text is far from felicitous. In any event, the following pages are addressed to those who value literature and who want to expand their engagement with literature by thinking through the mutually strengthening enhancements of translation and literary criticism. These pages provide also opportunity to consider some favourite authors once again. No matter how extensively we have studied any great writer, translation will give us new spaces for thinking about them.

3. Illustrated Historical Overview

Matters of direct survival must have instigated narration and language simultaneously. Indeed, narration itself is a translation of attitudes, beliefs, events and needs. The need to translate must have followed closely upon narration. By the time we reach recorded history and extant literature, literary history includes the history of translation, and does so with increasing explicitness. In traditional national literary histories, translation studies may seem overshadowed. However, every history has its leader who organizes translators to bring his court up to the perceived standards of his rivals. No Western history can overlook the impact of a period like the Renaissance or of texts like the Christian Bible or the *Communist Manifesto*. We might add that it is difficult and probably futile to separate the history of translation from the history of translation studies, as we are using the expression. As our discussion will soon make clear, conceptual issues arise almost automatically. Translations are needed; translations are criticized; translators are advised; finally, translations change lives.

Where literary criticism is concerned, the history of translation studies is essentially a record of successive guides to pleasing literary taste. As a matter of fact, translation theory, for example, should usually be punctuated with quotation marks, i.e. translation 'theory', since the 'theory' in translation studies, even now, is often not theoretical by twentieth-century standards. It is frequently a set of recommendations for adhering to accepted rhetorical practices as the recommender understands them. 'Accepted rhetorical practices' should be put in quotation marks also, for they are always a function of the taste of the rhetoricians issuing the pronouncement, and they are influenced in turn by the norms of the era.

Literature must have been translated for enhancing one group's cultural heritage at the expense of another's. Perhaps a kind of imperialism where the 'text' supported or solidified a territorial or lineal claim. Or perhaps a benign looting to bolster what was felt to be an inferior native patrimony. Or, less benignly, literature could have been translated as a pleasure commodity with a price; life in the case of Scheherazade, but minstrels, story-tellers must have been human trophies all along. The hypothetical and multiple origins must have many motives, and yet those motives were not too dissimilar from those of literary translation: using knowledge of language and skill of expression to satisfy some combination of power and desire. This would surely include the desire to share with

15

others, whether or not the others were expected to respond in a desired way. All in all, millennia later, the motives for translating literature may not be all that different. Like any form of collective memory trove, literary translation is a mediated record.

If we merely follow the fate of a single major literary work through its English metamorphoses, we have a microcosm of English literary history and literary language. (And we must remember that the work in question retains its 'major' classification in the canon largely because of translation.) Nearly a half century ago American Classicist Reuben Brower in 'Seven Agamemnons' (1959) – an essay that has itself become veritably canonical and is reprinted in his *Mirror on Mirror* (1974) – used seven versions of Aeschylus' *Agamemnon* (fifth century BC) to show how literary translations encapsulate the preferred serious literary styles of an era. Agamemnon successively speaks Elizabethan, Tudor, Augustan, Victorian and Modernist, with strong input from Seneca's Latin translation, and each generation of educated readers, from Shakespeare's to our own, have found the play has dramatic poetry fitting their own notion of what poetry is.

The impacts of literary styles in a language like English have been gradual but neither slow nor imperceptible. To over-simplify, after Chaucer reinstated English as a literary language, no major dynamic centre of English has known an upheaval that created a major rupture in the language. (We could say that the French Revolution of the 1790s and the Russian Revolution in 1917 affected French and Russian languages; certainly the Russian Revolution reduced the geographic terrain of French. The break-up of the Soviet Union in 1992 also broke up the over-arching translation policy that was to have united the country in a common language and culture from 1917 onwards.)

However, we need not go back five centuries or have recourse to dead languages, as did Brower, to illustrate both how a dominant style affects translation and how, as a translation receives criticism, it calls forth re-translation, by then due for changes anyway because of the ensuing changes in usage. Such changes include the expected shifts in grammar and lexicon in a dynamic language. They include also trends in literary rhetoric, the degree of literary involvement with social history, and the oscillations in prestige of translation in the target literature.

Let's look at two translations of Albert Camus's *L'Étranger* (1942): one by the British Modernist Stuart Gilbert (1945) and the other by the

American Postmodernist Matthew Ward (1988). Both translations are called *The Stranger*; both were sponsored by Knopf/Random House affiliates in the United States and are still available. These two translations are both fine in their own way, illustrating not only Modernist and Postmodernist taste but additionally the polar alternation between free and literal, target-oriented (domesticated) and source-oriented (foreignized), meaning-based (interpretive) and language-based (neoliteral). The alternations of these overlapping binary rhythms in the afterlife of a literary work have often taken over discussion in translation studies. But they are inevitable alternations within the larger overall diachronic alternations in literary history.

Gilbert's *The Stranger* has reached an incalculable number of English-language readers, chiefly students in the last year of secondary school or the first year of postsecondary education. In New York State the novel figured on the Reading List for the Regents examination, a requirement for all college-bound students. For nearly half a century these students in general literature and their instructors have heard 'each successive shot...' as 'another fateful rap on the door of [Meursault's] undoing' (1945:76) and have expected 'a huge crowd of spectators' to 'greet' him 'with howls of execration' (173). When their compatriots reading *L'Étranger* pointed out that the endings of Part I ('Et c'était comme quatre coups brefs que je frappais sur la porte du malheur', 80) and Part II ('qu'il y ait beaucoup de spectateurs le jour de mon exécution et qu'ils m'accueillent avec des cris de haine', 138) did not have quite the same referential ground as Gilbert's version, the English-language readers turned a deaf ear. The ear of the imagination certainly has to readjust to the lowered tone and deliberate repetition in Ward's retranslation: 'it was like knocking four quick times on the door of unhappiness' (59); 'I had only to wish that there be a large crowd of spectators the day of my execution and that they greet me with cries of hate' (123).

Camus, killed in an automobile accident in his late forties, wrote *L'Étranger* in his mid-twenties. Both his translators were older, with different kinds of life experience.

Both translators conceived their task by the literary norms of their own generation. Stuart Gilbert (1888-1969), who found a second career in translation after retiring from the British Civil Service in the 1920s, first came to scholarly notice with his *James Joyce's Ulysses* (1930), which was the guide that explained which Joyce section matched which

Homeric episode. By the time he came to *L'Étranger* he was in his late 50s, a friend and explicator of Joyce, and a seasoned translator whose Victorian education had been tempered by Modernism. He had translated Malraux, Martin du Gard, Saint-Exupéry and Simenon and he had published the first volume of Joyce's correspondence. Like most translators when they want to produce a text that sounds native to the literature of their own times, Gilbert appears to have conceived a target text on the basis of his own reading and made his translation conform to this interpretation. While his translation would be termed 'faithful', in terms of the contrasts mentioned above it is free, target-oriented (domesticated) and meaning-based (interpretive).

Matthew Ward (1951-1990) was born nearly a decade after *L'Étranger* was published. He would have had a Modernist education tempered by the Beat Generation and Postmodernism. An AIDS victim, he received a PEN Book-of-the Month Club award for this translation. Ward first encountered *L'Étranger* through Gilbert's translation, which he commended for "consistency", "earnestness" and as "an effort to make the text intelligible" (1988:vi). Ward's goal, as he put it, "was to venture further into the letter of Camus's novel, to capture what he said and how he said it, not what he meant. In theory, the latter should take care of itself" (vi). His translation is intentionally literal, source-oriented (foreignized) and language-based (neoliteral).

Camus presents a text that can be read like one of Gide's. The narrative surface is smooth, somewhat elliptical, at times lyrical. Reader collaboration is needed to interpret the significance of the narrative, but not, however, to complete it. We seem to have the entire narrative, and the matter can be left there. Gilbert's text reproduces that kind of effect, the kind of translation called seamless. He reproduces this effect by choosing a slightly poetic, educated lexicon and using the monologue rhythm of a coherent speaker. His narrative persona is too honest, but he has a certain earnest charm.

Of course, when Camus was writing, the narrative did not unfold smoothly and melodically onto the manuscript pages without difficult verbal choices and careful rewriting. If he had wanted to create a persona of earnest charm, he could have used French that would more closely correspond to Gilbert's choices. Ward, by looking for the more literal rendering, scrapes away some of the poetry and lets us see the roughness of the persona. This roughness, seen in lexical choices that are not as felicitous as Gilbert's, gives us the impression of seeing a quasi-final draft at the same time as the finished text.

If we compare two brief passages where the translators might normally be restricted by the amount of concrete detail in the text, we discover that Gilbert's translation, since target-oriented, manages to accommodate the presumed audience. And publishing history indicates that this accommodation was both profitable and accurate. However, his translation, as we shall see, does not have the same effect on the target audience as did Camus's text on the source audience, and such an effect, usually termed dynamic or functional equivalence, has long been assumed the goal of meaning-based translations. Ward's translation makes no such accommodation and yet probably does achieve an effect comparable to what happens in French. His backers at Knopf must have assumed that American readers were ready for Camus written with English words.

The first passage we shall consider is the description of a nursing home for French colonists of modest means, 84 kilometres from Algiers. The second passage occurs as Meursault, the novel's narrator and central character, adapts to his imprisonment.

Meursault notes when his mother's friends enter the wake after her death:

Je n'avais encore jamais remarqué à quel point les vieilles femmes pouvaient avoir du ventre. Les hommes étaient presque tous très maigres et tenaient des cannes. Ce qui me frappait dans leurs visages, c'est que je ne voyais pas leurs yeux, mais seulement une lueur sans éclat au milieu d'un nid de rides. Lorsqu'ils se sont assis, la plupart m'ont regardé et ont hoché la tête avec gêne, les lèvres toutes mangées par leur bouche sans dents, sans que je puisse savoir s'ils me saluaient ou s'il s'agissait d'un tic. (1942:28)

Gilbert makes the recollection as kindly as possible:

I'd never yet noticed what big paunches old women usually have. Most of the men, however, were as thin as rakes, and they all carried sticks. What struck me most about their faces was that one couldn't see their eyes, only a dull glow in a sort of nest of wrinkles.

On sitting down, they looked at me, and wagged their heads

awkwardly, their lips sucked in between their toothless gums. I couldn't decide if they were greeting me and trying to say something, or if it was due to some infirmity of age. (1945:10-11)

Did Gilbert realize these 'elderly' might belong to his own generation but had lacked his comfortable life? Was he trying to allay his readers' fear of ageing? In any event, Ward (undoubtedly already living under the death sentence of AIDS), does not mitigate Meursault's recollection:

I'd never noticed what huge stomachs old women can have. Almost all the men were skinny and carried canes. What struck me most about their faces was that I couldn't see their eyes, just a faint glimmer in a nest of wrinkles. When they'd sat down, most of them looked at me and nodded awkwardly, their lips sucked in by their toothless mouths, so that I couldn't tell if they were greeting me or if it was just a nervous tic. (10)

In Part II after Meursault has been in prison long enough to adjust to the routine, he summarizes the experience of imprisonment:

A part ces ennuis [lack of personal possessions, cigarettes, female company], je n'étais pas trop malheureux. Toute la question, encore une fois, était de tuer le temps. J'ai fini par ne plus m'ennuyer du tout à partir de l'instant où j'ai appris à me souvenir. [He details his regimen of remembrance and concludes:] J'ai compris alors qu'un homme qui n'aurait vécu qu'un seul jour pourrait sans peine vivre cent ans dans une prison. Il aurait assez de souvenirs pour ne pas s'ennuyer. Dans un sens, c'était un avantage. (1942:89)

Gilbert's Meursault is more explicit:

Except for these privations I wasn't too unhappy. Yet again, the whole problem was how to kill time. After a while, however, once I'd learned the trick of remembering things, I never had a moment's boredom. [Gilbert starts a new paragraph for the concluding moral:]
So I learned that even after a single day's experience of the outside world a man could easily live a hundred years in prison. He'd have laid up enough memories never to be bored. Obviously, in one way, this was a compensation. (1945:98-99)

It would be hard to press any great tonal difference in Ward's Meursault here; perhaps this is an instance where Ward believed he had American-ized the English:

> Apart from these annoyances, I wasn't too unhappy. Once again, the main problem was killing time. Eventually, once I learned how to remember things, I wasn't bored at all. [He keeps Camus's paragraphing, so the moral is not foregrounded:] I realized then that a man who had lived only one day could easily live for a hundred years in prison. He would have enough memories to keep him from being bored. In a way, it was an advantage. (1988:79)

The differences between the 1945 British translation and the 1988 Ameri-can translation are slight when isolated, but the accretion of differences leads to a difference in impact. That is, the fable or storyline has remained intact, but the narrator is not quite the same person. Gilbert's Meursault has fewer unappealing characteristics; thus he is more likely to be seen as an appealing victim. The aspect of the elderly in a wan electric light bemuses him. He explains he could not decide whether they were greet-ing him or *trying to say something* (four words added). He dismisses some disturbing sounds and gestures as due to *some infirmity of age*, certainly a vaguer and hence kinder concept than *un tic*. In contrast, Ward's Meursault, like Camus's, finds the elderly revolting. They look grotesque, and their attempt to greet him comes across as a *nervous tic*. As for the later prison routine, on 'how to kill time,' Gilbert's Meursault learns, rather constructively, a *trick* to *exercise* his memory. At first, he remembers, the exercise took *only a minute or two*. Just a *single* day in *the outside* (words added) would suffice for one to live in prison a hun-dred years. Ward's Meursault sounds more compulsive and, appropriately enough, stir-crazy. He will not stop talking. He has no more information on killing time than Camus's (i.e. at first remembering *était vite fait, didn't take long*). We do not doubt that he has developed such a strategy to cope with incarceration, but any healthy notion of mental self-discipline is dissipated – and thus in both Camus and Ward is followed logically – by Meursault confessing to pathological sleeping in the following paragraph.

The differences in persona and hence plot comes from Gilbert and Ward choosing different words and slightly different word orders and para-graphing. Gilbert is more idiomatic, a prime exemplar of the translator who affects invisibility. He is, paradoxically, more present. He has normalized the text. His translation fulfils the long-standing norm that a translation should sound as if written originally in the target language. His Meursault is an inadvertent rebel, a man who generally minded his own business, above all, worthy of our consideration, even sympathy, because of his total honesty and sincerity. Gilbert's *The Stranger* is an English novel about colonial Algiers in the late prewar period when roles of victim and victimized were beginning to blur. We do not read it, however, as a document of late colonial mentality.

In French literature Camus's *L'Étranger* is already archived as such a document, and Ward has brought that equivocal mentality into English by using what has subsequently been called a 'neoliteral' approach. Paradoxically, in updating the translation style he may have dated the novel, making it far less relevant to the 15-20 year-olds who formed its American audience. His Meursault, while barely a member of the middle class, is of French descent and is thus a *colon*, a member of the dominant French colonial caste in Algeria, who presumes on the law's disregard of the underclass without assuming the responsibilities (or at least their façade) of the overclass. The law, though, a quasi-autonomous set of texts and accretions (i.e. precedents) cannot disregard a fellow *colon* who, like Meursault, shoots a knife-bearing Arab four times after inflicting death. A man without remorse, who neither mourned his mother's death nor observed the proprieties of mourning, would not have shot in mere self-defense.

In short, when translation alters the first-person narrators, we readers receive different cues for establishing what we believe we think the *L'Étranger* means.

In terms of the relationship between translation and literary criticism, these two *Strangers* over a 50-year period suggest that the primary integrity of a text is its first-language textuality. The ensuing socio-political scene (its contentextuality) and the relations with other literary works and traditions (its intertextuality) continually subject it to apparent changes. Indeed, in time, the changes may become just as real as the originary 'meanings', which may require exegetical recall.

These last 50 years, a mere moment in Western literary history, still illustrate the 'heart-beat' of literary history, in itself a reflecting, recording part of socio-cultural history. I say 'heart-beat' because Western history since the Renaissance has the rhythms of the human heart. The overall cultural history of Western Europe and North America has alternated between modes of expanding and contracting, including and excluding. Modernism (like Neo-Classicism) tended to the contracting mode. Despite its development of new style norms, some of them like the Joycean and Proustian novel being expansive in themselves, its arbiters were quite emphatic about what the norms were and how important it was to adhere to them. Ezra Pound even used elliptical (mis)translation to support Imagism which in turn supported the appreciation of Mallarmé and Valéry's elliptical Symbolism. Surrealism is part of that deceptively open-looking restrictiveness. T. S. Eliot's Nobel Prize in 1948 retrospectively seems to have been the crowning culmination and effective conclusion of Modernism. This was three years after Gilbert's *Stranger*, which had begun a life of its own. But the translation's English expression was highly appropriate, because Camus wrote *L'Étranger* by the norms of pared-down style of the moraliste tradition of Gide and Mauriac. Gilbert's rhetorical norms, whatever we think of his interpretation, were English counterparts of this French tradition.

L'Étranger was one of the first accessible illustrations of what the absurd meant in the frame of Existentialism, and this theme shortly after exploded into Absurd Theatre and the New Novel (*Nouveau Roman*). The latter ushered in Postmodernism, although the critical Establishment floundered for a few years as it developed a counterpart methodology. What became clear was that culture had moved into expanding and including. American literary imperialism became as apparent as any political move by the United States, not as a domination but as co-option. (English has always been an open language, tolerant of 'misuse' and forever borrowing on its own.) Latin-American literature pushed aside the Iberian Peninsula. Francophone literature has received more attention than continental French literature. Nearly forty years after the death of Yeats and the corresponding end of Celtic Renaissance (and the end of Dublin as a dynamic language centre), the bilingual Samuel Beckett won the Nobel Prize in 1969. Was that award the apotheosis of the Absurd Theatre and the New Novel? Or an instance of atavism unrecognized at the time? In the popular press Beckett has been called the "Antijoyce of the modernist gospel" (Gates 1996:4). Did Claude Simon's Nobel in 1985 mark the end of the New Novel? In any event, the expansion continues. We are still living in the climate in which Ward translated.

Translation has, as always and once again, reflected both the momentum and norms of literary history.

4. The Recurring Rhythms

Cultural history, seen large or from afar, shows a continuous oscillation: balancing, realigning, balancing again. We could say balance gives way to imbalance (re-arrangement and conflict), which in turn leads to re-balance (self-correction, modification, integration). We could call the entire three-part process human or animate dynamics, because the process is a pattern repeated wherever there is the life force, the self-generating movement, of a living creature that will die – from individual human beings to social group to human history in the abstract. To this rhythm Hegel applied the labels of 'thesis', 'antithesis' and 'synthesis'. Yeats drew intersecting gyres of human history. I am using the simile of the beating heart. Certainly the movements deserve the epithet 'organic'. Whether systolic or diastolic, translation is part of the movement.

A cultural perspective such as Romanticism in the nineteenth century or Existentialism in the twentieth, like a long-lived human being, grows, flourishes, dominates, declines. It does not disappear, however; it becomes something else. It can be reactively incorporated into something else or it can proactively merge and/or modify. To stay with Romanticism, in retrospect, Romantic novels were pre-empted by Realism-Naturalism. Zola's characters, like Hugo's, are larger-than-life. In poetry, the prototypical Symbolist Baudelaire knew he was original but presumed he was following Hugo. A thesis, that is apparently opposed by an antithesis, becomes part of a synthesis, in its turn a new thesis.

The movements within these 'organisms' are even more life-like, however. While growing and declining, they are also and not necessarily in parallel fashion, expanding and contracting. Whether we visualize our heritage as coming down to us or rising up to us, in this study I have proposed that our collective cultural history forms a diachronic fluctuating movement throughout its course. At this point, let us simply call this fluctuating movement some kind of inner mobile that makes life energies alternate between expanding and contracting, including and excluding, bringing in and shutting out.

The moments of perfect equipoise for a period of high culture are finite (as we inevitably discover when we want to establish chronological boundaries) like the prime of a person of genius or beauty. Something in the balance of the dynamic is too delicate to stay as it is. Indeed, if it stays as it is, that very stay would become prejudicial. It is like holding the perfect pose for a photographer. A smile can become a grimace; a thoughtful look can become a vacant stare.

Since we have mentioned Yeats, did the Celtic Renaissance last until his death in January 1939? After all, his last poems and plays are among his best. Did it come to an end with the establishment of the Irish Free State in 1923? Or to take Surrealism, replete with warring camps and competing manifestos, did it end when Breton fell out with Aragon at the end of the twenties? Perhaps the Surreal impulse has always been with us. As for Naturalism, Zola laid claim to the first lines ever written.

Translation follows along usually in the wake of this diachronic fluctuating movement and usually seems to settle in a predictable niche. 'Follows' because what is being translated always comes first.

A 'translation' that comes first is an anomaly. Some may come first because they are single-work collections of what was published piecemeal in the first language: for example, when Tom Rockmore and Joseph Margolies edited *Heidegger and Nazism* by Victor Farias (1989), they joked that this was a translation for which there was no original. Then there are alleged translations that function as a preventive measure against censorship and/or as part of a work's humour. For example, Voltaire presents *Candide* as a translation from German, and Cervantes presents *Don Quixote* as a translation from Arabic. We do not take such claims seriously. It has been a long, long time since casual readers have bothered to read the 'translators' notes' in *Candide* and *Don Quixote*.

As anomalies, full-fledged pseudotranslations have a more complex history. They deserve to be taken up case-by-case. For our discussion, the case of the Scot poet and linguist James MacPherson (1738-96) is germane because his alleged translations of an alleged third-century Celtic bard, Ossian, were taken seriously as literature only in translation. In the British Isles, the publication of these pseudotranslations in 1760-63 was controversial on the very issue of authenticity, i.e. were there originals for these translations? But for French and German literature, the prose epics were read avidly and had not only a direct influence but also an indirect impact that was widespread and profound, particularly when transmuted into the self-pitying prose declamations of Goethe's *Werther* (1774) and Chateaubriand's *René* (1802). Both Goethe and Chateaubriand could read Ossian in English: Chateaubriand translated Milton's *Paradise Lost*; Goethe inserts his own translations from Ossian into Werther and Lotte's final tryst, where 200 or so lines of translation take the place of dialogue and action. (True to the nature of translating, Werther's translation is somewhat longer than MacPherson's.) The relationship is compounded since English translators of *Werther* and *René* take their diction cues from Macpherson (just as this *Axël* translator took her cues from Milton).

As we shall have cause to observe later, the readers' knowledge that they are reading translations can work either to the advantage or disadvantage of the work. The case of Ossian would indicate that readers gave the texts the benefit of the doubt. Readers, usually without articulating their attitude, think something like the following: If the text sounds this good in translation, it must be marvellous beyond imagining in the original. This 'benefit' is itself dubious since it is posited on the inferiority of a translation. (On the other hand, even with the same data or observations, readers can be hypercritical, concentrating on what the translator must have done wrong, rather on what beauties come through despite the change in the languages involved.) With Goethe and Chateaubriand, I am inclined to surmise that, as non-native readers of English, they were less critical than they would have been of literature in their own languages.

In terms of our simile, this is not an irregular or syncopated heart beat. The pseudotranslation created a beneficent shock that accelerated the alternation from restrictive to expansive first in German literature and later in French literature.

Translation can also be used considerably more knowingly to bring a literature out of lethargy or veritable cardiac arrest. Germaine Necker de Staël (1766-1817) intended her somewhat polemical literary criticism as in *De la littérature* (1800) to accelerate such an alternation in French literature from restrictive to expansive by promoting literatures of other languages, chiefly German. She herself, it may be noted in passing, uses translation as a strategy in her novel *Corinne* (1807): the heroine is an Italian poet whom we imagine marvellously eloquent from the cues given in the French 'translation'. In the first years of the twentieth century, Ezra Pound (1885-1972) accelerated the movement from expansive to restrictive with ostensible translations from Chinese and Provençal (as in *Cathay*, 1915).

Such developments intensify the degree of fluctuation, sometimes ushering in counter directions, sometimes creating nearly simultaneous directions, with surface disturbances making it hard to see the pattern. The picture can be extremely blurred (more like a chest X-ray than an electrocardiogram) where translations are concerned, since aside from the personalities trying to change literary norms like de Staël or Pound, translators (and in the English-speaking world, at least) editors, above all, are trying to follow established norms. In fact, translators and their editors during the past three decades have tended to be conservative in their usage and especially wary of the vanguard. They often confess to following their own urge to 'improve', i.e. normalize, the text they are translating; editors may consider it their professional duty to normalize.

Such basically benign conservatism comes naturally to translators. In the final analysis, no matter how sweeping the checklists they make for themselves, they must rely on their ear, on what sounds right. Or as Douglas Robinson has said in *The Translators's Turn* (1991), on their 'gut', on what feels right. This means they must rely on remembering what they have heard or how something is said. In either case, they are relying on their memory. If the what and the how of what they are translating is entirely new, their memory may be an unreliable resource. If what is new begins to flourish, upsetting the balance, then translators will begin hearing the new. The translators may still be hostile, and editors may still be resistant, but there will be new norms and/or new potential choices in circulation. For example, French Postmodernists have elicited neoliteral translations that can be read stereoscopically. Derrida's French had a new sound that his American translators chose to mimic in English. When readers, who found Gayatri Spivak's *Of Grammatology* (1976) strange, returned to the French, they found little clarification in *De la grammatologie* (1967). It, too, sounded strange. The French text gave meanings a new twist, and English could replicate that twist only by perceptible literalness. Further, and more essential for my thesis, those reading both French and English texts had and have an added dimension of meaning in the mental space between the French and English words. Alphonso Lingis, translator of Emmanual Levinas (1906-95), is quite open about his strategy. He says in his preface to *Otherwise than Being* (1981), his translation of *L'Autrement qu'être* (1974), that "the present English version, more than most philosophical translations, is a transposition of the original text, and does not wish to sever its dependence on and subordination to it" (xxxviii).

At this point we see as an overlay the tensions of the binary oppositions mentioned in the last chapter: free vs literal, target-oriented (domesticated) vs source-oriented (foreignized), meaning-based (interpretive) vs language-based (neoliteral). By and large, the translation tensions can be predicted in terms of our heartbeat simile.

When a literature is in a phase of expanding and including, it is likely to be looking for new subjects, new themes and new sounds. This phase may well make it receptive to translations that show their foreign origins. Madame de Staël and her circle at Coppet certainly thought of themselves as capable of accommodating the foreign and alien. However, if the translated works sound too alien, they may have reduced reception, and herein enters the phantom of the projected reader. The marketplace or the patronage system, which can include state censorship, publishing economics and dominant mores, will influence the tolerable degree of strangeness. If a translation sounds too strange, it may not be accepted. With German and English literature read in French translation during Romanticism, the tolerance range was not extensive. But by the time we come to Baudelaire's touted translations of Poe, we are dealing with literal, source-oriented, language-based translations, extremely deferential. Indeed, Baudelaire seems perfectly suited for the task by taste and temperament. In retrospect, Baudelaire's Poe translations harmonize well with the expanded content and varieties of forms permitted by Symbolism-Decadence.

Yet Mallarmé, who initiates the amalgam of Symbolism with Modernism, which was selectively restrictive, translated Poe also. We may extrapolate that Mallarmé, whatever he felt when labouring over material he found essentially untranslatable, created a Poe who used words as artifacts. And whatever reverence the generations of Yeats, Pound or Eliot felt toward the French Symbolists, it did not extend to the Symbolist enthusiasm for Poe, in or out of translation.

(It is not that translation ceased to be important before World War I. On the contrary: Pound translated; he and Eliot were adept in foreign languages. Yeats, albeit monolingual, appreciated the resonance of Gaelic and translated Greek and Hindi with a collaborator. Yeats, who went to French performances of Jarry and Villiers de l'Isle-Adam, believed that he understood a great deal even though he could not recognize the words.)

Literature in English traditionally stays longer in an expanding and inclusive phase than the French. It is tempting to generalize that English is typically expansive, and French is typically restrictive. After all, English is a more open language than French. A Germanic language with a long stretch of Anglo-Norman>French overlay, English seems to encourage users almost endemically or inherently to supplement by borrowing, coining, inventing. There has been no counterpart of the French Academy to prescribe usage. Furthermore, we are so happy to have our interlocutors speak English that we tolerate considerable variance in all language features. Whatever sociolinguistic factors have contributed – the sometime sweep of the British Empire, the sometime American dominance after World War II, the ease with which the language is learned (if it is), the delight with which native English speakers accommodate non-native speakers, the convenience of English as a lingua franca – our lexicographers and grammarians record usage far more than they prescribe it.

Yet – our first proviso: This can be obscured by the power of the editor in Anglo-American publishing or even be sent in reverse. Whatever the phase in the cultural heart beat, the generic translation editor will prefer poems that sound like poems (presumably what was vanguard when the editor was an undergraduate English major), natural idioms and frequently only the foreignness of proper nouns. Since only the translator and possibly the author will know what the text looked like before copy-editing, readers generally will not suspect how much a published translation can deviate from the translation submitted. In 1994, the first year of the MLA Scaglione Translation competition – I had the privilege of serving on this committee from 1994 to 1997 – all the novels submitted by one major American publishing house, regardless of language of origin, sounded as if they had been written by the same author.

Yet – a second proviso: For masterworks or ancient and medieval works, the philological tradition in translation, the interlinear translation, may remain nearly unchanged. Today facing-page translations may have replaced the interlinear. This is a boon to scholars, especially with ancient works where the actual text has been established with some difficulty or Classical Greek and Latin texts that figure importantly in disciplines outside classical philology. (Heidegger sent American philosophers of the Postmodernist 'continental' camp to Greek.) These are instances where the original-language text has considerable prestige and the translator risks less criticism in being literal. But the facing-page format permits a translator considerable licence, because the format engages monitoring by bilingual readers. We have seen this in poetry translations of the past thirty years. It is up to bilingual readers to 'correct' the translations. The neoliteral phase of the past two or so decades occurred at many American academic presses for translation in the humanities and social sciences precisely because of the emphasis on the role of language in the disciplines concerned. All such types of translating demarcate the boundaries of text and translation and hence the in-between area to which we shall devote the rest of this study.

We shall see fluctuating boundaries when we turn from literary history in its broad oscillations to literary criticism of specific texts at specific times. We shall see that as a critical tool, a translation will yield up according to the critical approach used.

5. Baudelaire: Poet and Translator

We have mentioned Baudelaire's famous re-creation of Poe. It was translation in the usual sense. Baudelaire was enraptured with Poe. He saw in him a mirror image or, perhaps, his American persona. He brought his English up to the task, devoting four years of study before undertaking the project. Both the translating and prior study coincided with the composition of his earlier poems. *Histoires extraordinaires* was ready for publication in 1853; *Les Fleurs du mal*, in 1857. We by no means accept the judgment of Baudelaire's biographer Joanna Richardson that "Poe wrote with vulgar smartness; Baudelaire translated him into classic French" (1994:150). Both wrote effectively by the standards of their respective languages in the mid-nineteenth century. Poe, who remained outside the New England nexus that dominated American literature, did not receive nearly as thorough a formal education as the New England writers; although he knew foreign languages and cultures less, he displayed them more. He made his content Western, but stateless; his rhetoric, learned and allusive with continental references. His dialogues have the diction of stage melodrama. He already sounds exotic, and the cultural specificity of, say, Thoreau or Hawthorne, which would require a translator to acquire some knowledge of the United States, is, by design, missing in Poe. Could we even go as far as to say that he sounds in English as if already translated from French?

In any event, for a writer like Baudelaire, who received a traditional *lycée* education, we may speculate that the Poe persona was rhetorically and lexically liberating. Much as Baudelaire admired the writers of the short-lived French Romanticism, his favourite novel was Sainte-Beuve's *Volupté* (1834) and he was an early promoter of Flaubert's *Madame Bovary*, pilloried the same year as *Les Fleurs du mal*. *Volupté* is a complacent, rhetorically ornate castigation of sensuality; *Madame Bovary* is a morality demonstrating the self-destructiveness of sensuality. *Volupté* displays metaphors and similes; *Madame Bovary* relies on metonyms. Either novel could reinforce Baudelaire's own environmentally imprinted respect for mesure, which we could define in his case as a careful avoidance of extremes and a preference for the understated, both in art forms and material culture. Poe gave Baudelaire simultaneously the means to indulge his flamboyance and to control it. French is simply more conservative and traditional than

English. Lexically, Poe allowed Baudelaire full expression of desperation, morbidity, excess; full expression, in short, of the extravagance of feelings beyond the strictures of high bourgeois taste exemplified by his mother and stepfather. Poe allowed him to make verbal choices which the reader would not expect. Rhetorically, Poe's prose permitted Baudelaire to express himself rhythmically but with licence.

We can pick a passage from the two writers for stereoscopic reading nearly at random and verify that Baudelaire visualized what Poe intended and he transcribed the sight as deferentially as French permitted. If I say that the sight is less clearcut in French or that the French picture is slightly blurred, this probably means that as a native English bilingual reader I have sharper visual referents for English. Indeed, as we shall see, Baudelaire compensates to keep a comparably palpable ambiguity. As for the sound, Poe's deliberate, somewhat Latinate nineteenth-century periodization goes into French more smoothly than contemporary English might.

For examples, we can take a few sentences from the first paragraph of 'The Fall of the House of Usher' ('La Chute de la Maison Usher'). I shall back-translate Baudelaire in brackets quite literally, frequently even calquing syntax, to make the interliminal more apparent. In the first sentence Baudelaire follows closely but moves the time-setting nouns to the beginning:

> During the whole of a dull, dark, and soundless day in the autumn
> of the year,

> Pendant toute une journée d'automne, journée fulgineuse, sombre et
> muette,
> [Throughout a long autumn day, sooty, sombre and mute,]

(Should we object that *autumn of the year* analogizes with middle age? or that *fulgineuse/sooty* adds a hue and texture?)

> When the clouds hung oppressively low in the heavens,

> où les nuages pesaient lourds et bas dans le ciel,
> [where the clouds weighed heavy and low in the sky,]

> I had been passing alone, on horseback, through a singularly dreary
> tract of country;

> j'avais traversé seul et à cheval une étendue de pays singulièrement lugubre,
> [I had crossed alone and on horseback a singularly lugubrious stretch of countryside,]

(Should we object here that *traversé/crossing*, instead of *passing... through*, may change the location of the Usher house from within a dreary tract to something on the other side of it? With both Poe and Baudelaire it is clear that the narrator is travelling by himself. I should say that neither makes it clear whether the speaker was the only one crossing this tract.)

> and at length found myself, as the shades of evening drew on, within view of the melancholy House of Usher.

> et enfin, comme les ombres du soir approchaient, je me trouvai en vue de la mélancholique Maison Usher.
> [and finally, as the shadows of evening approached, I found myself within view of the melancholic House of Usher.]

The term *shades* has the pun potentiality of ghosts, so with *ombres* Baudelaire must obscure, if not cut out, an allusion. However, Baudelaire compensates with *approchaient*, which is more threatening than *drew on*. When we consider that it has been overcast all day, *drew on* simply suggests overall darkening like pulling down a shade; *approchaient*, 'approached', either comes on the horizon like a tornado or comes down on the narrator, threatening to enclose him. After all, Baudelaire is the poet who compares the sky to a manhole cover in 'Au lecteur'. In this sentence and the next, Poe achieves the diction of hymns. We would not expect Baudelaire to reproduce this, even if he recognized it.

> I know not how it was —

> Je ne sais comment cela se fit —
> [I don't know how it happened —]

> but, with the first glimpse of the building, a sense of insufferable gloom invaded my spirit.

> mais, au premier coup d'œil que je jetais sur le bâtiment un sentiment d'insupportable tristesse pénétra mon âme.
> [but from the first glance I cast upon the building a feeling of intolerable sadness penetrated my soul.]

Poe would have used *soul* if he had wanted to, but the French *esprit* – 'mind' and 'spirit') would have been subject to misinterpretation.

The next sentence may give us an instance of Baudelaire stepping up the tone of the French – perhaps to compensate for *tristesse* being a little weak for *gloom* in the preceding sentence. Or because we now respond with alarm to *volupté*, perhaps in part because of Baudelaire himself: the word has nearly entered English, and with strong, unambiguous sexual connotations.

> I say insufferable; for the feeling was unrelieved by any of that half-pleasurable, because poetic, sentiment, with which the mind usually receives even the sternest natural images of the desolate or terrible.

> Je dis insupportable, car cette tristesse n'était nullement tempérée par une parcelle de ce sentiment dont l'essence poétique fait presque une volupté, et dont l'âme est généralement saisie en face des images naturelles les plus sombres de la desolation et de la terreur. [I say intolerable because this sadness was in no way tempered by a hint of tiniest amount of that feeling which the poetic essence makes almost voluptuous and which generally takes hold of the soul facing the most sombre images of desolation and terror.]

Again, Poe, whose narrator is trying to discipline himself to objective re-collection, avoids *soul*.

In the next sentence, which compares the visual impression made by the house to the let-down following opium, Baudelaire uses both *regardais* and *éprouvais* to render *I looked* and *with*. Baudelaire also refers to coming out of opium with more detail and less poetry (suggesting more first-hand experience).

> I looked upon the scene before me – upon the mere house, and the simple landscape features of the domain – upon the bleak walls, – upon the vacant eyelike windows – upon a few rank sedges – and upon a few white trunks of decayed trees – with an utter depression of soul which I can compare to no earthly sensation more properly than to the after-dream of the reveller upon opium – the bitter lapse into everyday life – the hideous dropping off of the veil.

Je regardais le tableau placé devant moi, et, rien qu'à voir la maison
et la perspective caractéristique de ce domaine – les murs qui
avaient froids
[I looked at the scene placed before me, and, from nothing but
seeing the house and the characteristic perspective of that domain
– the walls that were cold.]

(A *tableau* is more a stage set than simple scene; Poe's *bleak* is bare and
forbidding, not 'cold'; Poe does not even use *clammy*)

– les fenêtres semblables à des yeux distraits – quelques bouquets
de joncs vigoureux [the windows like distracted eyes—a few clumps
of vigorous rushes].

(Poe's *a few rank sedges* is a veritable oxymoron. Baudelaire's 'rewriting'
may be an improvement.)

– troncs blancs et déperis – j'éprouvais cet entier affaissement
d'âme, qui parmi les sensations terrestres, ne peut se mieux
comparer qu'à l'arrière-rêverie du mangeur d'opium
[white and wasted trunks – I experienced that total weakening of
soul, which among earthly sensations, can best be compared only
to the after-dreaming of the opium-eater.]

(Poe's *reveller* suggests at least temporary enjoyment; an *eater* simply
ingests.)

– à son navrant retour à la vie journalière – à l'horrible et lente
retraite du voile.
[to his nightmarish return to daily life – to the horrible and slow
withdrawing of the veil.]

(The phrase *slow and horrible withdrawing* has a different duration.)

Poe explains further having recourse to 'the sublime', a favoured term
of Romantics:

There was an iciness, a sinking, a sickening of the heart – an
unredeemed dreariness of thought which no goading of the imagination could torture into aught of the sublime.

C'était une glace au cœur, un abattement, un malaise – une irrémédiable tristesse de pensée qu'aucun aiguillon de l'imagination ne pouvait raviver ni pousser au grand.
[There was ice in the heart, an enfeeblement, a sickening – an unredeemable sadness of thought that no goad of the imagination could revive or push to something grand.]

(*Raviver*, 'revive', and *pousser*, 'push' or perhaps 'impell', are weaker than *torture*, not to mention the beloved *sublime* and the pun of *aught/ ought/naught*).

Throughout the translation, Baudelaire has set provisional French boundaries for a reader's interliminal response. As a reader, Baudelaire has so much authority that we may feel initially that his is the only authentic expansion of Poe's text. But what Baudelaire has provided in fact is another set of bornes for our own interliminal spaces. When we backtranslated Baudelaire, we did not spontaneously duplicate Poe. What we shall achieve if we complete the tale is a collaborative, if only partially articulated, text of our own.

By and large, Baudelaire has made Poe's tale more reasonable, even while adding the spirituality of a soul. It is a good translation, and it is certainly in good taste by conservative standards. We find such refinement wherever we read Poe and Baudelaire stereoscopically.

Conservative good taste suggests that a triage is taking place in the translating. When Baudelaire came to his own poetry, including his prose poems, he was ready for further triage, keeping effective lexical units in metrically exacting prosodic forms.

We might have expected Baudelaire to translate Poe's poetry. It may simply have been a matter of timing. Poe's collected *Tales of the Grotesque and Arabesque* was ready for distribution in 1840; his *The Raven and Other Poems* in 1845. Baudelaire encountered Poe first in translation: 'Le Chat noir' ('The Black Cat') by Isabelle Meunier in the January 1847 issue of *La Démocratie pacifique*. His quasi-intuitive identification began at that point. He proceeded to study English; he ordered Poe's works from London on 15 October 1851. Of course, in an extended sense, some of his later poems may well 'translate' his experiences with Poe; for example, Mary Ann Caws (1983) has seen a connection between Poe's 'The Oval Portrait' ('Le Portrait oval') and Baudelaire's 'Le Fantôme' sequence (1860): 'Les Ténèbres','Le Parfum', 'Le Cadre', and 'Le Portrait'. The final word on the Poe-Baudelaire nexus will probably never be uttered (for two of the best early essays, see Block 1977, 1984).

Yet Poe was not the only source. In one of his few identified poetry translations, Baudelaire in 'Le Guignon' (1851) presents a fascinating transformation of one of Longfellow's most often misunderstood poems 'The Psalm of Life'. In Longfellow's brisk octosyllabic lines, trochees muffle embittered resignation. Here is stanza 3: 'Art is long, and Time is fleeting,/ And our hearts, though stout and brave,/Still, like muffled drums, are beating/Funeral marches to the grave'. Baudelaire keeps the short lines but French prosody would make trochees undetectable (there are underlying iambs here). His verse reinforces sober reflections: 'L'Art est long et le Temps est court' (Baudelaire, line 4; Longfellow, line 13; Ars longa, vita brevis is the Latin translation from Hippocrates: Ho bios brakus, hè de tèchné makra).... 'Mon coeur, comme un tambour voilé,/Va battant des marches funèbres'. (We shall touch again on Baudelaire's indebtedness to Longfellow in the following chapter.) In this poem Baudelaire borrows also from Thomas Gray's 'Elegy Written in a Country Church Yard' (1751), getting his third and fourth stanza from the 14th stanza of Gray's poem. It is no coincidence that this Gray stanza is Poe's epigraph to 'The Tell-Tale Heart', which Baudelaire translated as 'Le Cœur révélateur'. Baudelaire shortens Gray's iambic pentameters ('Full many a gem of purest ray serene/The dark unfathom'd caves of ocean bear;/Full many a flower is born to blush unseen,/And waste its sweetness on the desert air'.): 'Maint joyau dort enseveli/Dans les ténèbres et l'oubli,/ Bien loin des pioches et des sondes; Mainte fleur épanche à regret/Son parfum doux comme un secret/ Dans les solitudes profondes'.

Let us close by recalling that Baudelaire was enraptured by Wagner also, seeking out Wagner's writings as well as his librettos. What he says about Wagner is like a commentary on how he intended to translate Poe. He did not, however, take on German. The passages he quotes at length in 'Richard Wagner et Tannhauser à Paris'(1859-61) are from French translations, some based not on German but on English translations from the German. He lifts several paragraphs verbatim on the interconnections of the arts in *Lettre sur la musique* where Wagner summarizes his earlier publications. (Baudelaire also cites Lizst, a Hungarian writing in French and fluent in German.) His opportunities to hear Wagner performed were few, but he found in what Wagner wrote a corroboration for the artist as critic. "It is impossible", he concludes, "that a poet not be a critic. The reader will thus not be surprised that I consider the poet as the best critic of all" (1976:793, my translation). Certainly when he immersed himself in Poe his critical faculties were alert, and in this piece on Wagner he lets us see the direction – the restrictive direction – his translating would take: "Poetry existed, it was the first [art] to establish itself, and it has engendered the study of rules" (793, my translation). He is true to his own precepts. His Poe would be refined, and the resulting translated text as well.

6. Baudelaire: Poet Translated

Baudelaire's own reception outside France has depended more upon bilingual readers than on translators. It would be difficult to claim that his poems had received a truly satisfactory English translation yet, although every now and then some poet manages a few good isolated lines. We can reasonably hypothesize that Arthur Symons (1865-1945), who accompanied Yeats to performances of Jarry's *Ubu Roi* and Villiers de l'Isle-Adam's *Axël*, translated as he read. His popularization of Symbolism in *The Symbolist Movement in Literature* (1899) helped make it an international idiom. He limited himself to themes, and his own translations and variations are singularly disappointing, leading to the further hypothesis that he read from within some kind of personal fog. But there is hardly any doubt that what he said about Symbolism had an effect.

Symons' view of Symbolism was picked up, amplified, and given a far more scholarly and far-reaching context by another bilingual reader, Edmund Wilson, an American professor whose *Axel's Castle* (1931) integrated the Poe-Baudelaire ricochet into a persuasive causality. Wilson alternates paraphrases and quotations in French from Baudelaire and Mallarmé to explain, presumably, how such disparate individual writers as Yeats, Gertrude Stein, Proust, Joyce, Mallarmé, Rimbaud and Valéry can be linked together in a Symbolism (we would now say Modernism) that recasts the Romantic anti-mechanistic credo. His title is indebted to Axel, the hero of Villiers de l'Isle-Adam's play by the same name. Axel, who prefers the idea of things to the thing itself, persuades Sarah, his fated beloved, to join him in suicide in the castle vault: 'Vivre? les serviteurs feront cela pour nous' (literally: 'Live? the servants will do that for us'). In the play, this rhetorical question is somewhat downplayed, being in the next-to-last paragraph of a very long speech. It will be submerged further by the nuptial song that Axel's page Ukko begins off-stage. However, it is from H. P. R. Finberg's 1924 translation that Wilson extracts his quotations. Wilson stops short, however, of quoting the pronouncement that implicates all allegedly superior persons: 'As for living, our servants will do that for us' (170).

It was not until Finberg's translation that Yeats could actually read *Axel*, and we infer from his introduction, where he goes back to his published recollections of the 1894 performance he saw with Symons, that he was a bit taken back by his own impressionability. In any event, when he put together *A Vision* in 1928, he was inclined to review the play ironically. One member of the foursome waiting for Michael Robartes is a young woman who calls herself Denise de l'Isle-Adam because she was reading *Axël* in bed the night she fell in love. She summarizes (*A Vision* 1961:42): "Axel and Sarah decide to die rather than possess one another. He talks of her hair as full of the odour of dead rose leaves – a pretty phrase – a phrase I would like somebody to say to me; and then comes the famous sentence: 'As for living, our servants will do that for us'". Denise (or Yeats) has rearranged the dialogue. It is Sarah who describes her hair to Axel as a place where 'tu respirerais l'esprit des roses mortes' (you would inhale the spirit of dead roses) (*Axël* 1960:230) [cf. my own interpretative, normalizing translation – published (1970:155): "Let me veil you in my hair so you may inhale the attar of roses of all time"] .

Although the examples given in our purview have been French to and from English, translations of Baudelaire also affected other literatures as well. It is hardly an overstatement to say that the case of Baudelaire in German was responsible for a landmark in translation theory.

This is because translating Baudelaire undoubtedly crystallized Walter Benjamin's thoughts on translating. Although his Baudelaire translations may be too literal – and in that respect too true to his theory (or too revelatory of his poetic gifts) – to have superseded Stefan George's, the experience gave him an opportunity to confirm his developing views on literary and sacred language. His role as an intermediary has fluctuated, of course, even since Steiner's recuperation of him in *After Babel* (1975). His importance is still in the foreground in literary criticism. (In the North American version of 'continental' or post-Heideggerian philosophy, Benjamin is now part of the pantheon.)

Walter Benjamin (1899-1940) was a translator as well as a literary critic and historian. His 1923 essay 'The Task of the Translator' (*Charles Baudelaire. Tableaux parisiens. Deutsche Übertragung mit einem Vorwort über die Aufgabe des Übersetzers*) brought the support of speculative philosophy and speculative theories of language to translation. Words, somewhat reminiscent of the Kabbalistic tradition, began to have autonomy and resonance of their own, a status I should like to call mythic. Benjamin's essay returns our discussion to the oscillating movement within the heartbeat of cultural history. Benjamin's conception of translation is so extreme in its source orientation (foreignized) and so language-based that we can say of those who follow him that they are neoliteral. In 1916

Benjamin had written an essay on the nature of language ('On Language as Such'/*Über die Sprache überhaupt und über die Sprache des Menschen*) that should be considered in tandem with 'The Task of the Translator'. We should bear in mind also that Benjamin was simultaneously translating Baudelaire and working on a social history of Baudelaire's era.

Oversimplified, Benjamin argued that Baudelaire was the first translator of *Les Fleurs du mal* because he translated into poetic language the repercussions of experiences that could have had a distinctly non-verbal nature or origin. But what I have called 'a distinctly non-verbal nature' Benjamin, in On Language as Such', calls the 'language of things': "The linguistic being of things is their language; this proposition applied to man means: the linguistic being of man is his language. Which signifies: man communicates his own mental being in his language... by naming other things' (trans. Edmund Jephcott 1978:317) ["Das sprachliche Wesen der Dinge ist ihre Sprache; dieser Satz auf den Menschen angewandt besagt: Das sprachliche Wesen des Menschen ist seine Sprache .... Der Mensch teilt also seine eigenes geistiges Wesen ... mit, indem er alle anderen Dinge benennt" (1916:11-12)]. A single author-translator, in this instance Baudelaire, would be unlikely to get the non-human language fully translated. Therefore, literature needs many translators in the same language and different languages, so that readers can put together the originary message. It follows – at least for Benjamin – that the most literal translation, using lexical cognates and syntactic calques where possible, would be the most satisfactory. Such a translation, unlikely to be flowing and smooth, would be the most likely to let the original – the pre-verbal, what was subsequently put into language – be glimpsed or heard.

Benjamin's translations of *Les Fleurs du mal* follow his precepts. Such precepts, however, did not, in my opinion, lead to felicitous translations (although such precepts *could* have: Richard Wilbur's *Molière*, replete with cognates and calques, crackles and pops). Benjamin's translations require a bilingual, or nearly bilingual reader, who knows Baudelaire rather well and can appreciate the French echoing through the German. On the other hand, a poet whom Benjamin considered one of the greatest German translators, Stefan George (1868-1933), welcomed by Mallarmé's Paris circle in 1889, created *Die Blumen des Bösen* (1891), a translation of 115 Baudelaire poems. These are elegant and moving with a melody of their own. The faint echo of Baudelaire is an enhancement of appreciation, but readers need not hear it to appreciate the poems. Indeed, George's translations have been advanced as an example of the potential equality or superiority of translation. In his epochal *Truth and Method* of 1960, Hans-Georg Gadamer claims that George's translations infuse Baudelaire's lines with a singular new healthiness: "In rare cases of really fine translation the loss can be made good or even lead to gain – think, for example, of how Baudelaire's *Les Fleurs du mal* seem to have acquired an odd new vigour in Stefan George's version" (trans. Garrett Barden and John Cumming 1975:348).

Let us take a single sonnet for our examples, Baudelaire's 'Recueillement' (1861). Further, since there is no definitive English translation for this particular sonnet (although I share the consensus that Richard Howard's is our best) we can compare George's and Benjamin's translations with an English plain prose 'control'.

Recueillement
Sois sage, ô ma Douleur, et tiens-toi plus tranquille.
Tu réclamais le Soir; il descend; le voici:
Une atmosphère obscure enveloppe la ville,
Aux uns portant la paix, aux autres le souci.

Pendant que des mortels la multitude vile,
Sous le fouet du Plaisir, ce bourreau sans merci,
Va cueillir des remords dans la fête servile,
Ma Douleur, donne-moi la main; viens par ici,

Loin d'eux. Vois se pencher les défuntes Années,
Sur les balcons du ciel, en robes surannées;
Surgir du fond des eaux le Regret souriant;
Le Soleil moribond s'endormir sous une arche,
Et, comme un long linceul traînant à l'Orient,
Entends ma chère, la douce Nuit qui marche.

George, Sammlung	Benjamin, Vorbereitung
Sei ruhig, o mein leid, und klage schwächer,	Gemach mein Schmerz und rege du dich minder
Du riefst den abend nieder, sieh er kam!	Der Abend den du anriefst sinkt und glückt
Ein dunkler odem legt sich auf die dächer –	Dunkelheit umhüllet die Stadt gelinder
Dem einen bringt er ruh dem andren gram	Die jenen friedlich macht und den bedrückt
Mag sich der sterblichen gemeiner haufen	Und wenn der taube Scharm der Menschenkinder
Gepeitscht vom taumel, dem gestrengen herrn,	Dass er sich Reu in seinen Freuden pflückt
Bei knechtischem gelag den ekel kaufen . .	Von Lust gepeitscht wird seinem argen Schinder
Mein leid, gib mir die hand! von ihnen fern!	Gib mir die Hand mein Schmerz lass uns entrückt
Ganz fern!. . .sieh wie die toten jahre droben	Gewahren wie sich von Altanen droben
An himmel winken mit verblichnen roben.	Die alten Jahre neigen in den Roben

Die reue lächelnd auf den wassern schwebt.	Wie lächelnder Verzicht sichaufhebt aus der Flut
Die sonne sterbend hinter bögen breitet.	Die Sonne durch den Brückenbogen leitet
Ein langes leintuch sich im osten hebt.	Und wie ein Leichentuch das übern Osten ruht
Horch teure! horch! die nacht die leise schreitet!	Vernimm vernimm sie doch die süsse Nacht die schreitet

As titles and subject indicators, Baudelaire's *Recueillement* suggests collecting [oneself] to achieve composure. George's *Sammlung* uses equivalent roots for an equivalent meaning, while with *Vorbereitung* Benjamin has 'preparation' [for something]. He prepares us for his interpretation. We will now take apart each line: the first German line is George's; the second, Benjamin's. The English interlinears are mine.

Sois sage, ô ma Douleur, et tiens-toi plus tranquille.   **A.fem.12- syllable**
Be prudent, my Sorrow, and stay calm.

Baudelaire uses traditional alexandrine lines (iambic hexameter) in the sonnet. They verge on being soft or indeterminate, however, because their content encourages conversational reading, even though the tradition imposes declamation à la Comédie française. When read as if in conversation, instead of recitation, Baudelaire's lines are nearly iambic. This feature de-emphasizes certain syllables and is an advantage for German (and English) translators because the translation convention of converting French 12-syllable alexandrines to 10-syllable iambic pentameters often forces translators into ellipses. Both George and Benjamin soften their iambic pentameters with a final extra weak syllable.

G.   Sei ruhig, o mein leid, und klage schwächer,   **A.fem.11 syllables**
     Be still, o my sorrow, and complain more faintly,
B.   Gemach mein Schmerz und rege du dich minder   **A.fem.11 syllables**
     Softly my Pain and move less

Capitalized, *Douleur* is a feminine personification, recalling Poe's Psyche who wandered with the poet to the tomb of Ulalume. George uses a neuter noun, not capitalized, despite the German convention of capitalizing all nouns. George typically flouts this convention – and would eventually modify standard punctuation – when composing poetry. The choice of *leid* ('Sorrow') suggests a more obsessive mental state (and less a personification) with physical repercussions, which the poet is trying to bring under control. (For a bilingual reader, the lack of capitalization adds to the

43

flow, since there is no slight pause to accommodate the capitalization of a common noun.) George's is an interpretive translation. Benjamin uses a masculine noun which has primary physical connotations: *Schmerz* ('Pain'). It would be difficult to say that he visualized a male companion as in 'The Love Song of J. Alfred Prufrock' (i.e. 'Let us go then, you and I') or even that he thinks of a personification at all, since this is normal German capitalization, but it sounds more as if he had a sore limb which he protects by not moving. Neither German translation has a Poe echo, but George compensates by spiritual intimacy achieved prosodically by reproducing Baudelaire's two caesural pauses, which made the line conversational.

	Tu réclamais le Soir; il descend; le voici:	**B. masc. 12 syllables**
	You called for evening; look it's falling now.[1]	
G.	Du riefst den abend nieder, sieh er kam!	**B. masc. 10 syllables**
	You called down the evening, see it came!	
B.	Der Abend den du anriefst sinkt und glückt	**B. masc. 10 syllables**
	The evening you called sinks and thrives.	

Both German translators submerge the caesural pauses, George, effectively, within diction somewhat more consoling than Baudelaire's; Benjamin, prosaically in a relative clause. Is it felicitous that 'evening' is the same gender in both languages? *Le Soir* would be a natural companion for *la [ma] Douleur*. Because of the tenses used, there may be some question as to whether it is precisely the same time of day in all three lines. For George, it is already evening. Perhaps that is what Benjamin means also with *und glückt*, suggesting that evening has taken over.

	Une atmosphère obscure enveloppe la ville,	**A.fem. 12 syllables**
	An obscuring atmosphere envelops the city,	

Because of all the interfacing vowels, Baudelaire's line may seem longer than it is. It can be read conversationally as loose iambic.

G.	Ein dunkler odem legt sich auf die dächer –	**A.fem.11 syllables**
	A dark air touches down upon the roofs –	

This is an instance where George simultaneously adds and subtracts

---

[1] At the close of *Endgame*, Beckett has Hamm translate, 'You CRIED for night;it comes – ... It FALLS: now cry in darkness.... You cried for night; it falls; now cry in darkness' (83).

specificity: we infer from the following lines that we are dealing with an inhabited area, but the persona only points out dark mist on the roofs. Benjamin stays closer.

B.	Dunkelheit umhüllet die Stadt gelinder Darkness gently envelopes the city	**A.fem. 11 syllables**
	Aux uns portant la paix, aux autres le souci. To some bringing peace, to others care.	**B.masc. 12 syllables**
G.	Dem einen bringt er ruh dem andren gram To one it/he brings calm to another grief.	**B.masc. 9 syllables**
B.	Die jenen friedlich macht und den bedrückt Makes this one peaceful and that one anxious	**B.masc. 10 syllables**

The German translators have no problem phrases here. The only quandary is mine: should I insist on the masculine gender of evening (*it* vs *he* in the lines above) to make some point about George's companionship and/or sexual orientation? It would not have occurred to me to translate Baudelaire's pronominal references to *le Soir* ('evening') as *he*.

Here, however, the two German translators diverge. George moves to a Shakespearean rhyme scheme, while Benjamin keeps to Baudelaire's Petrarchan scheme:

	Pendant que des mortels la multitude vile, While the vile horde of mortals	**A.fem.12 syllables**
G.	Mag sich der sterblichen gemeiner haufen May the common mortal hordes	**C.fem.11 syllables**
B.	Und wenn der taube Scharm der Menschenkinder And when the mortal swarm of sons of men	**A.fem.11syllables**
	Sous le fouet du Plaisir, ce bourreau sans merci, Beneath the lash of Pleasure, pitiless hangman,	**B.masc.13 syllables**
G.	Gepeitscht vom taumel, dem gestrengen herrn, Whipped to reeling, to the harsh taskmaster,	**D.fem. 9 syllables**
B.	Dass er sich Reu in seinen Freuden pflückt That gathers remorse in his/their joys	**B.masc.10 syllables**
	Va cueillir des remords dans la fête servile, Goes gathering remorse in base festivities,	**A.fem.12 syllables**

G.   Bei knechtischem gelag den ekel kaufen ...   **C.fem.11 syllables**
      In slavish orgy purchase surfeit ...
B.   Von Lust gepeitscht wird seinem argen Schinder **B.fem. 10 syllables**
      Is whipped by Lust for his wrathful Taskmaster

Benjamin has effected the greatest adjustment, moving clauses, not a bad strategy in itself, but giving us a possessive pronoun (*seinem*, which grammatically could refer either to *Lust* or the joys (*Freuden*) it procures. Both George and Benjamin make the behaviour deplored worse than that described by Baudelaire's persona. Baudelaire does depict *Plaisir* as forceful and compelling as *volupté*, a noun associated with him, but a word he does not use here. On the contrary, his language speaks to compulsive socializing that causes regret by wasting time. *Plaisir* is a masculine noun. As a personification it has a malefic influence on the persona; this influence calls into existence *Douleur*, a feminine noun. She co-habits or co-exists with or in the persona. Both German translators heighten the tone in interpreting, and Benjamin can interject a hint of *Schadenfreude*, perhaps Dr. Freud!

    Ma Douleur, donne-moi la main; viens par ici,   **B.masc.12 syllables**
    My Sorrow, give me your hand; come this way,
G.   Mein leid, gib mir die hand! von ihnen fern!   **D.fem. 10 syllables**
    My sorrow, give me your hand! Leave them far behind!
B.   Gib mir die Hand mein Schmerz lass uns entrückt **B.masc.10 syllables**
    Give me your hand, my Pain, let us away

Baudelaire's Poesque Psyche *Douleur* depends on this personification in a poem that is almost an allegory. George's line is quite euphonic. Moving to c/d/c/d may have liberated his rhyming – one may wonder about the neuter entity with whom he wishes to walk hand in hand. Benjamin keeps a/b/a/b and has a concluding line that may have an infelicitous sound to some ears. Neither keeps the enjambment that makes Baudelaire's sonnet flow from octave to sestet:

    Loin d'eux. Vois se pencher les défuntes Années,   **C.fem.12 syllables**
    Far from them. See the bygone Years leaning

Vois (imperative 'see') is critical, governing *se pencher* ('to lean') in line 9,

Surgir ('surge') in line 11, and *s'endormir* ('go to sleep') in line 12. George has *sieh* ('see') govern *droben* ('lean') in line 9. His lines 11 and 12 are separate declarative sentences. Although Benjamin eschews punctuation, his lines 11 and 12 are separate declarative sentences also. *Gewahren wie* ('Note how') seems like the wrong register for this sonnet.

G.   Ganz fern! ... sieh wie die toten jahre droben   **E.fem.11 syllables**
     As far as possible! ... see how the dead years lean

B.   Gewahren wie sich von Altanen droben   **C.fem. 11 syllables**
     Note how from the heights lean

     Sur les balcons du ciel, en robes surannées;   **C.fem.11 syllables**
     On the balconies of heaven, in gowns of yesteryear;

G.   An himmel winken mit verblichnen roben.   **E.fem.11 syllables**
     From heaven to beckon in faded gowns.

B.   Die alten Jahre neigen in den Roben   **C.fem.11 syllables**
     Old Years nodding in gowns

My own interpretation of this poem led me to use *heaven* instead of *sky*. If we have to do with a fantasy memory, as I believe is the case with Baudelaire, then *heaven* is probably more appropriate. If we have to do with a vision, as may be the way George interprets the line, I should have used *sky*, at least for *himmel*.

     Surgir du fond des eaux le Regret souriant;   **D.masc.12 syllables**
     See smiling Regret surge from the waters' depths,

G.   Die reue lächelnd auf den wassern schwebt.   **F.masc. 9 syllables**
     Remorse smiling rises from the waves

B.   Wie lächelnder Verzicht sich aufhebt aus der Flut   **D.masc.12 syllables**
     How smiling Resignation rises from the flood

This tercet, with its compression of memories personified as women, is easy to feel and hard to explain. Various scenes in which the persona remembers his mother in his fantasy childhood? If the persona imagines himself on such balconies, the melancholy he feels is not unpleasant melancholy. That is, *Regret*, his own, a masculine noun, smiles. George interprets much as I have; indeed, I may have interpreted thus because of George. There is no 'beckoning' in Baudelaire, but the persona may feel an attraction because he asks his *Douleur* to join him in gazing at these years past. Benjamin's *neigen* ('nod') may derive from his having visualized George's *winken* ('beckon'). And Benjamin has found remorse tempered by resignation, rather than regret arising from the confrontation of memories.

Le Soleil moribond s'endormir sous une arche,	**E.fem.12/13 syllables**
The dying Sun go to sleep beneath an arch,	
G. Die sonne sterbend hinter bögen breitet.	**G.fem. 11 syllables**
The dying sun spreads out behind the arch.	
B. Die Sonne durch den Brückenbogen gleitet	**E.fem. 11 syllables**
The sun glides through the bridge arch	
Et, comme un long linceul traînant à l'Orient,	**D.masc. 11/12 syllables**
And like a long shroud drifting in the East,	
G. Ein langes leintuch sich im osten hebt.	**F.masc. 10 syllables**
A long linen cloth rises in the east.	
B. Und wie ein Leichentuch das übern Osten ruht	**D.masc.12 syllables**
And like a shroud the upper east rests	
Entends ma chère, la douce Nuit qui marche.	**E.fem.11 syllables**
Hear, my beloved, the gentle Night approach.	
G. Horch teure! horch! die nacht die leise schreitet!	**G.fem. 11 syllables**
Hark dearest! hark! the gentle night is striding!	
B. Vernimm vernimm sie doch die süsse	**E.fem.13 syllables**
Nacht die schreitet	
Hear hear then the sweet night striding	

In plain prose Baudelaire is telling his dear *Douleur* that the steps of Night sound like a shroud being dragged from the East. Baudelaire's directions, however, are deliberately confusing. *Traînant à* would usually be 'drifting to or in the East'. Is it a rustling? Should we visualize Night dragging a veil or train behind her? Such pictures are not far-fetched. After all, the sun is falling asleep beneath an arch. This could be a building or a bridge, as the persona and his Douleur watch. Thus, the trailing cloud of the sunset would be dark wisps in the East. Here is a clear instance where the two German translators help with complementary pictures. George sees a sun going down in a dispersal of light, and in the east the visual effects of an extended shroud, following naturally upon a dying sun. Does his persona hear more noise in the final line? 'Stride' vs 'walk'. Or does his use of *Horch* ('hark') signal a hand raised to silence, since only if we keep very still can we hear night coming on? Benjamin's tercet glosses George's. The 'arch' is specifically that of a bridge, and the upper eastern sky rests like a shroud, suggesting clouds that have turned dark. Under these conditions the persona enjoins *Schmerz* to hear the night coming. It would seem that each German translator, personally knowing Paris well, put himself in the situation of the persona of the poem.

Taken together, these texts illustrate Benjamin's belief that the poet is the first translator and that many a translation is needed to render with even partial completeness the original inspiration. As readers, we profit, according to this perspective, from having all five translations. Since none is inaccurate, we receive a fuller approximation of whatever might have been Baudelaire's melancholia at twilight. Further, since each set a different interliminal boundary, we have become aware of nearly limitless possibilities within this sonnet. Like Yeats's 'Sailing to Byzantium', 'Recueillement' has a stable core of meaning encoded, but a widening and shifting circumference that has an expanding inner space. The successive circumferences, albeit demarcated by changing rhetorics, semantics and cultures made visible by translation, are by no means fixed. If we translate into another language, another English control, we will intuit yet another opening upon Benjamin's pure language of pre-verbal expression.

We could categorize George's translation as target-oriented, domesticated, interpretive, meaning-based; Benjamin's as source-oriented, foreignized, language-based. Yet such categorizing would critically oversimplify. George, like Pound in American literature, was trying to give his native-language poetry both a new sound and a new look. He was relying on readers' tolerance for strangeness in translation, so while he was target-oriented, he was still foreignizing. To appreciate George one does not, however, need to have Baudelaire's French ringing in one's head. Benjamin relies on well-read bilingual readers. Whether or not readers accept his choices, the French echoes through them and must be heard by readers (who, otherwise, will wonder at Baudelaire's reputation in world literature).

If it is qualitatively better to engage in literary criticism from the inside looking out, rather than from the outside looking in, both George and Benjamin moved inside the subject (knower) of the poems, operating as critics via translation. Both identified with Baudelaire's persona. The paradox here is that Benjamin's neoliteral strategy of obvious dictionary meanings and closely imitative rhyme scheme keeps a reader, who is not German/French bilingual, on the outside. Such a reader can decode the poem but hardly experience it.

Inasmuch as I have avoided the technical lexicon of literary criticism, it may not have been obvious that I was making use of several critical strategies simultaneously.

In terms of tradition, I have just put forward an *explication de texte*, using six texts in three languages instead of one text in a single language. (The texts are Baudelaire's, George's, Benjamin's and my own plain-prose controls for each.) In Anglo-American criticism the strategy would be identified with New Criticism, promoted by such teachers of literature as Cleanth Brooks, Robert Penn Warren and René Wellek. That is, our discussion, apart from a few asides (as when I noted that both Benjamin and George knew Paris well) stayed within the confines of the texts. Externally, on the outside looking in, I labelled the prosody. Internally, on the inside looking out, I speculated on the emotional repercussions of the lexicon and the prosody. In every instance, the German and the English helped me understand and categorize the French.

At the same time our discussion was observing practices that have a more current nomenclature. I was moving in and out of the texts as would be expected in Deconstruction. Indeed, I allowed our discussion to move further from the text than explication or New Criticism would advocate when I posed a rhetorical question about the *défuntes Années in robes surannées*, linking the image to Baudelaire's fantasizing about his mother. If my implicit supposition is likely, these Years are 'fantasy memories'. I ascribe these female personifications to memories of balcony evenings that never took place in actuality. Baudelaire's widowed mother remarried when he was seven, and his stepfather did not want the boy to interfere with their privacy by living with them. The out-of-date clothing might truly have been what his mother would have worn 25 or 30 years earlier, but Charles as an older child or adolescent would not have seen her wearing them very often. Here they are material symbols of make-believe evenings together. But even in daydreams, they provided the bittersweet comfort of pseudo-recollections. Both George's and Benjamin's translations reinforce such a reading and bring us to the borders of biographical criticism. Our discussion did not move into variations of biographical criticisms, such as psychological (pre-Freudian like Sainte-Beuve's) or psychoanalytical (Freudian and post-Freudian).

Still, that rhetorical question could be pursued, as could the observations made regarding grammatical gender. Whether from habituation or design or both, Baudelaire uses masculine and feminine nouns as male and female personifications in traditional roles of active man and reactive woman. *Douleur* (fem.), the companion of the male poet's persona, had called for *Soir* (masc.). Such an escort would be a dubious protector. The couple (the poet and *Douleur*) could be delivered into the hands of *Plaisir* (masc.). The *défuntes Années* (fem.) are a comforting sight. Their appearance calls up the virile response of a smiling *Regret* (masc.). As a result of the passing hour and the 'language' of the memories (the *défuntes Années*), the dying *Soleil* (masc.) falls asleep. In the distance, too far away to be seen, can be heard *Nuit* (fem.) who is douce ('gentle', 'sweet'). She will take the place of *Soir*. If *Nuit* were coming in rustling leaves or lapping waves, we might find her Shakespearean, bringing the sleep that knits the ravelled sleeve of care. But since she arrives with the soughing of a trailing shroud, we can reasonably conjecture that *Nuit* brings the final sleep of death.

In this respect (a very literal *regard* in both French and English senses because Baudelaire and George use *vois* and *sieh*) George's translation allows the same concluding death wish. George's *leintuch* ('linen cloth' or 'bedsheet') follows the derivation of Baudelaire's *linceul* (from *lin*, 'linen') and is more subtle, since Night could be trailing billows of gossamer linen. George may well have remembered Baudelaire's literary source, the 'trailing garments' and 'sable skirts' in Longfellow's 'Hymn to the Night'. Benjamin, who uses *gewahren* ('be aware of', especially in a situation of risk) and *Leichentuch* (literally 'corpse cloth cover'), makes the death wish unambiguous; he may have been influenced by knowing that Baudelaire was translating Poe at the time. Yet in not following Baudelaire's genders throughout, George and Benjamin have, in my opinion, downplayed the eroticism inherent in this death wish.

Both translators let us move our discussion into literary history and genetic criticism (i.e. working from origins). We know from Baudelaire's own testimony that he borrowed from Longfellow's collection *Voices of the Night* (1839). If we are cued, we can hear the swish and rustle of Longfellow's much more alluring female personification. Within Baudelaire's corpus, there is 'Le Crépuscule du soir' (1851) and the prose analogue

(1855-61) from *Le Spleen de Paris*. We may owe the sexual complementarity of the poet, *Douleur* and *Nuit*, as opposed to the sexual paralleling of *soir/crépuscule*, to Longfellow's example.

Baudelaire's standing in both his own literature and comparative literature is securely canonical. Longfellow, who, unlike Baudelaire, was immensely popular in his own times, is hardly even read except by specialists in nineteenth-century American literature. It is too much to hope that a doctoral student in French will track down a reference to Longfellow and start a revival of interest in Longfellow, even restore him to the pantheon of premier English translators, where he most assuredly belongs. However, this miscellaneous footnote to literary history and genetic criticism brings us to both Benjamin and the criticism his revival has received through the past two or so decades from sometime proponents of the polysystem.

The relation to Benjamin is obvious and would be so even if Benjamin had not been a Baudelaire scholar, for what we have seen in our review of the German translations by George and Benjamin is that they have given his works an 'afterlife'. They have provided complementarity and reinforcement, letting us perhaps hear or see more distinctly the pre-verbal poem of Baudelaire's inspiration. Indeed, the procession of one unsatisfactory English-language translation after another may make Baudelaire an especially persistent shade like the creatures caught in Yeats's Dreaming-Back, returning again and again to the sites of their betrayal in order to find peace in the after-world.

Now, I recognize that those who originally proposed the polysystem have largely gone on to descriptive translation studies and that many of them pay little attention to serious literature. Others, however, have taken up their strategies and continued to use them in comparative literature. Scholars working with those strategies will see Baudelaire as an extremely rich and complex case of inter-language intertextuality. As a translating reader he absorbed serious German literature (Wagner) and ultimately popular American literature (Poe, Longfellow). He became the polar star of Symbolism/Decadence, which functioned directly in serious literature in English-speaking and German-speaking milieux. (In Spanish-speaking as well, although this has not been part of our discussion.) We see this in American and British Modernism and note that Baudelaire is still revered by Postmodernism. Indirectly, perhaps nearly imperceptibly he, like Poe, has contributed to the repeated incursions of Decadence into the popular arts that comprise a larger segment of a complex literary system (why not say 'polysystem'? it is less cumbersome than 'descriptive translation studies') than serious literature. These popular forms include television, bestseller gothic and applied arts, all translations of a sort.

Yet, in my opinion, after 25 years the methods of descriptive translation studies brought to us by the polysystem have not enabled us to get inside literature. Such description can provide literary critics and historians with a wealth of data, but not an alternative mode of literary criticism. For example, a polysystem study of repeated translations of a single work over a period of time can provide a lexical and syntactic record of the changes in taste and ideology, since translations usually follow prevailing norms. Such patient research can be immensely useful to literary historians. It does not, however, lead a reader into a text for the most profound experience of it. Certainly it does not provide us with new internal mental spaces for thinking about a text or the experience that inspired it.

Some variety of hermeneutic approach is certain to remain the most rewarding. This could be a daring deconstructionist cross-reading such as that Jacques Derrida advances in *Donner le temps* (1991, *Given Time I: the Gift of Money*, 1992) where he gives Baudelaire's 28th prose poem in *Le Spleen de Paris* a reading that cannot be appreciated without recourse to both Peggy Kamuf's accompanying translation and Edward Kaplan's *The Parisian Prowler* (1989). Here Derrida has brought to bear on a literary text the Deconstructionist strategy that he developed to the furthest pole of comprehensibility in his reading of Heidegger in *Geschlecht II*, faithfully rendered in English by John P. Leavey, Jr., where it could be said that French (or English) is only the matrix holding together verbalized ricochets among English, French, German, Greek and Latin (1987). There are two matters to note here: first and most important, Derrida wrote this essay after 'Des tours de Babel' (1980, 1985), which was his answer to George Steiner's *After Babel* (1975). (*After Babel*, as has been noted, inaugurates the recuperation of Walter Benjamin's 'The Task of the Translator', and 'Des tours de Babel' is Derrida's reading of the same essay.) Second, Derrida places that undefinable bundle of concepts called 'meaning' in the interliminal mental space between the source and target texts.

That interliminal space is essentially where our discussion of 'Recueillement' has taken place. It is the 'space we think in' when we participate in such a stereoscopic reading, i.e. a reading that moves back and forth among source texts and one or more target texts. The best literary criticism, I propose, is that which uncovers (or, as Heideggerians would say, 'unconceals'), then 'translates' in the Benjaminian sense (I have used 'verbalizes') the interliminal richness, and finally points out the harmony or disjunction among the texts. This gives us a full, but never complete, enhanced explication weaving within the back-and-forth whatever socio-historical, biographical and psychological factors seem necessary. The terminology can use any Ism in vogue.

We have been weaving together a sense of 'Recueillement' like the strands of a complex braid (a French braid, in fact). While language dynamism should make us beware of codification, we need not forego system and scholarship for free association. Let us pursue the interliminal further with concluding cases of stereoscopic reading, hardly possible except where translations, traditionally defined, are available.

7. Turning to Prose

Of course, it is widely recognized that the gnomic encapsulations of poetry require especially attentive reading even in the first language. To judge by sales, that fictitious composite 'the general reader' probably reads little poetry after leaving formal schooling, certainly little poetry in translation. But those same 'general readers' who love to read because they want to add to their personal stores of experience while being entertained and who love to learn but want the material accessible – these same readers make other, not unreasonable, assumptions about prose. We all do. No matter how much time we have spent translating or teaching works in translation, we read whatever it is as the 'real thing'. (Bilingual short-story anthologies, as far as I can tell, are used chiefly by graduate students reviving their foreign-language reading skills.) Yet we should all recognize that the text in translation can hardly be the thing-in-itself because it cannot be the same thing. It is a circumference of interpretation around the axis of the first-language text and as such functions as a facsimile. (Of course, it is the most efficient vehicle available for reaching the axis.)

Thus, if we apply to prose the procedures we have just used with poetry, we shall, as with poetry, enhance our experience of it. That is, by articulating the affective, semantic space between the first text as we understand it and the translation, which records how the translator understood it, we combine the two texts, expanding and deepening each.

When teaching literature in translation it is preferable to work with an English that is familiar to the students (e.g. American English for North American students), but for the purposes of literary criticism any English that is thoroughly comprehensible will suffice. Indeed, if it is removed in time and sounds slightly non-idiomatic, it may let us add more adumbration. Let us look at three examples: Charles Kenneth Scott Moncrieff's 1928 translation of Stendhal's *La Chartreuse de Parme* (1838-40), Robert Baldick's 1964 translation of Flaubert's *L'Education sentimentale* (1869) and Carmen Swoffer-Penna's 1996 translation of Baudelaire's *La Fanfarlo* (1847, 1869).

Scott Moncrieff (1889-1930), whose Proust translations have received more attention than his other translations, was an interpretive translator of considerable flair. He translated from Latin (The Letters of Abelard and Heloise), Old French (The Song of Roland), and Italian (two minor plays by Pirandello) as well as all of Stendhal's major works.

Bilingual readers who cavil at his choices are obliged to recognize that they are apt, sometimes inspired. Consider, for example, just some of the titles he gave to Proust's masterpieces like *Remembrance of Times Past* for *À la recherche du temps perdu* ('On the Search for Lost Time') or *Within a Budding Grove* for *À l'ombre des jeunes filles en fleur* ('In the Shadow of Blooming Girls'). We have to acknowledge that his brainstorms circumvent some translation problems. *Cities of the Plain* for *Sodome et Gomorrah* is positively inspired. We should be grateful not only for his patience but for his intuition for appropriate allusions to British literature. Patience must have been called for with *La Chartreuse de Parme* as well. He barely begins his task before encountering some untranslatable terms in the opening chapter 'Milan en 1796'. The narrator refers to 'la volupté naturelle aux pays méridionaux' and recalls 'la joie folle, la gaieté, la volupté, l'oubli de tous les sentiments tristes, ou seulement raisonnables' (1972, 76) during the French Occupation of Milan from 15 May 1796 to April 1799. These three terms – *La joie folle, la gaieté, la volupté* – are listed because they are sequentially related states: shared 'heedless glee' among individuals leads to collective 'gaiety' which in turn leads to simultaneous exhilaration and release of 'delectation'. Moncrieff finesses the translation problem with 'This thirst for pleasure natural in southern countries .... This frenzied joy, this gaiety, this thirst for pleasure, this tendency to forget every sad or even reasonable feeling ...'. (1925:9-10). We can hardly fault him for not foreseeing the aura *volupté* has in present-day North American criticism, but we could have expected him to know about the invitation Baudelaire proffered Marie Dabrun in both poetry and prose: 'Là, tout n'est qu'ordre et beauté,/Luxe, calme et volupté....Tout y parlerait/À l'âme en secret/Sa douce langue natale' ('There, all is order and beauty,/ Luxuriousness, calm, and voluptuousness .... Everything there would speak secretly to the soul in its gentle native tongue'; 1975:53-54). Certainly Baudelaire knew *La Chartreuse de Parme*. However, when we juxtapose these passages we increase, if only for the reading of this particular novel, the referential range of *volupté*; 'thirst for pleasure' is active, a state of desire that requires fulfilment, while *volupté* is a state where pleasurable sensations are received.

As Stendhal pushes his protagonist into the intrigue that will provoke the manslaughter blighting his career, he lets us into this hapless womanizer's thoughts at the beginning of Chapter XI:

En descendant l'escalier tournant de ce taudis infâme, Fabrice était plein de componction: je ne suis point changé, se disait-il; toutes mes belles résolutions prises au bord de notre lac quand je voyais la vie d'un œil si philosophique se sont envolées.

Moncrieff believes he should heighten the Italian colour in this novel; hence Fabrice becomes Fabrizio. However, what is notable here is his use of a word that has to be seen juxtaposed next to Stendhal's French choice; otherwise, the sentence will be misread:

As he made his way down the winding staircase of this foul rookery, Fabrizio was filled with compunction. 'I have not altered in the least', he said to himself; 'all the fine resolutions I made on the shore of our lake when I looked at life with so philosophic an eye, have gone to the winds.'

American readers seeing only the English will think Mariette lived in a place where birds live: a rookery. The association with bird droppings and nest litter is not inappropriate. But it is only the cue of *taudis in-fâme* ('notorious tenement') that sends us to an unabridged dictionary to learn that 'rookery' is linked to 'to rook or cheat' — and that the translation is apt. (Frankly, in the next clause a literal *changed* would have been more subtle than *altered*, a synonym for 'neutered', an unsexing that priesthood did not effect with Fabrice.) Stendhal continues,

Mon âme était hors de son assiette ordinaire, tout cela était un rêve et disparaît devant l'austère réalité.

Moncrieff, of course, has to interpret, and here, too, the English is a cue to readers of French to check a dictionary. What we had learned for *assiette* ('plate') sounds silly:

My mind has lost its normal balance; the whole thing was a dream, and vanishes before the stern reality.

'Soul' has become *mind*, as if Moncrieff thought Stendhal should have used *esprit*, but rendering *assiette*, the 'seat' in equitation to describe a mental state is challenging. Perhaps 'My soul [we are dealing with a priest] had lost its bearings'. Probably more objectionable is Moncrieff's use of the present perfect (*has lost*) for the imperfect because Fabrice is referring to a state that had some duration but is now over and done with (I had to use the pluperfect).

> Ce serait le moment d'agir, se dit Fabrice en rentrant au palais Sanseverina sur les onze heures du soir.

> 'Now would be the time for action,' he told himself as he entered the *palazzo* [again, heightening the Italian colour] Sanseverina about eleven o'clock that evening.

Moncrieff has neatly adjusted the tenses in shifting to indirect discourse.

> Mais ce fut en vain qu'il chercha dans son cœur le courage de parler avec cette sincérité sublime qui lui semblait si facile la nuit qu'il passa aux rives du lac de Côme.

> But it was in vain that he sought in his heart for the courage to speak with that sublime sincerity which had seemed to him so easy, the night he spent by the shore of the Lake of Como.

We wonder why an editor did not streamline the *of the Lake of Como* to *of Lake Como*. Stendhal's duple rhythm is not replicable in triple rhythm.

> Je vais fâcher la personne que j'aime le mieux au monde; si je parle, j'aurai l'air d'un mauvais comédien; je ne vaux réellement quelque chose que dans de certains moments d'exaltation. (185)

> I am going to vex the person whom I love best in the world; if I speak, I shall simply seem to be jesting in the worst of taste; I am not worth anything, really, except in certain moments of exaltation. (218)

Vex sounds a little quaint, but *jesting in the worst of taste* borders on mistranslation. What Fabrice does not want to 'seem' is 'like a bad actor'. We do not know whether following good intentions would have been either laughable or insulting because he followed his womanizing reflexes instead.

By and large, the translation is excellent (although my students have been unanimous that Moncrieff has lowered the level of the rhetoric). In one of those rare passages where the narrator lets genuine sympathy for humankind intrude, Stendhal's and Moncrieff's texts are veritably isomorphic. This is in Chapter XXI when Fabrice's escape from the Parma prison was to be facilitated by the drug-induced illness of Fabio Conti, the prison warden:

Fabio Conti était un geôlier toujours inquiet, toujours malheur-eux, voyant toujours en songe quelqu'un de ses prisonniers lui échapper: il était abhorré de tout ce qui était dans la citadelle; mais le malheur inspirant les mêmes résolutions à tous les hommes, les pauvres prisonniers, ceux-là mêmes qui étaient enchaînés dans des cachots hauts de trois pieds, larges de trois pieds et de huit pieds de longueur et où ils ne pouvaient se tenir debout ou assis, tous les prisonniers, même ceux-là, dis-je, eurent l'idée de faire chanter à leur frais un *Te Deum* lorsqu'ils surent que leur gouverneur était hors de danger. Deux ou trois de ces malheureux firent des sonnets en l'honneur de Fabio Conti. Oh! effet du malheur sur ces hommes! Que celui qui les blâme soit conduit par sa destinée à passer un an dans un cachot haut de trois pieds, avec huit onces de pain par jour et *jeûnant* les vendredis. (374-75)

Fabio Conti was a gaoler who was always uneasy, always unhap-py, always seeing in his dreams one of his prisoners escaping: he was loathed by everyone in the citadel; but misfortune inspiring the same resolutions in all men, the poor prisoners, even those who were chained in dungeons three feet high, three feet wide and eight feet long, in which they could neither stand nor sit, all the prisoners, even these, I say, had the idea of ordering a *Te Deum* to be sung at their own expense, when they knew that their governor was out of danger. Two or three of these wretches composed sonnets in honour of Fabio Conti. Oh, the effect of misery upon men! May he who would blame them be led by his destiny to spend a year in a cell three feet high, with eight ounces of bread a day and *fasting* on Fridays! (174-5)

Stendhal uses *malheur* and *malheureux* twice each, whereas Moncrieff uses sequentially *unhappy, misfortune, wretches* and *misery*. Does this demonstrate French polysemic subtlety or English lexical richness? Or both simultaneously? In any event, here and elsewhere in these representa-tive comparisons, the translator meaningfully contributed to the space between our bilingual reading and his. He forced us to read more carefully.

We nearly always face the interlingual jousting of French polysemy and English univocality when reading as bilinguals. When it comes to demonstrating what French can do, Flaubert is perhaps an even better exemplar than Stendhal. His prose yields so much in monolingual readings that we adjust our expectations of a translation. We know that the sheer momentum of plot and characterization will sustain a translation. On the other hand, we expect to lose the subtle word plays provided by polysemy. Let us take a few frequently cited passages from *L'Éducation sentimentale* (1869). The translator Robert Baldick (1927-1972) is noted for his scholarship in late nineteenth-century French literature. His translation credits include Huysmans' *À rebours* (*Against Nature*), the Goncourt brothers, and Villiers de l'Isle-Adam's *Contes cruels*. He translated Flaubert's *Trois Contes* (*Three Tales*) as well as *Sentimental Education*.

In the first chapter, on the boat trip home, the main character Frédéric sees among the passengers Madame Arnoux, who will crystallize the Madonna of his love life. After he has seen her, the narrative camera turns to what he sees. The landscape is substantially the same:

Une plaine s'étendait à droite; à gauche un herbage allait doucement rejoindre une colline, où l'on apercevait des vignobles, des noyers, un moulin dans la verdure, et des petits chemins au delà, formant des zigzags sur la roche blanche qui touchait au bord du ciel. (1869:9)

A plain stretched away to the right; on the left a meadow sloped gently up to a hill, on which vineyards and walnut-trees could be distinguished, with a mill in the midst of the greenery. Further up, paths zigzagged across the white rock which seemed to touch the sky. (1964:20-21)

Despite the same landscape, the camera movement is somewhat modified because Flaubert, using *l'on* ('one') keeps an agent who perceives, namely Frédéric himself. He sees the green of the field (it is 15 September) going towards a hill, and once he is focused on the hill he sees buildings of rural life and from there sights a natural monument. From Frédéric's distance, man-made paths have wrapped and tied the boulder. Baldick's translation is accurate but initially more neutral, introducing this sight with the passive *could be distinguished*. However, he hints at a viewing agent when he closes with *seemed to touch the sky*. The juxtaposition shows us what Frédéric saw (Flaubert) and what someone trying to see things from Frédéric's angle saw (Baldick). The nature of English imposes removal of any gendered anthropomorphism, allowing for no male grassy patch (*un herbage*) going to join again (*rejoindre*) a female hillock (*une colline*), no pre-Freudian mill (*un moulin*) surrounded by bushy greenery (*la verdure*), counterpointed by a boulder (*la roche*) touching the boundary of the sky (*le ciel*).

The fact remains that the combination of an agent (*l'on*) and the covert sexuality of French grammatical gender provides the reader with a transition to the indirect discourse of the next sentence. An English reader has to make an inference:

> Quel bonheur de monter côte à côte, le bras autour de sa taille, pendant que sa robe balayerait les feuilles jaunies, en écoutant sa voix, sous le rayonnement de ses yeux! Le bateau pouvait s'arrêter, ils n'avaient qu'à descendre; et cette chose bien simple n'était plus facile, cependant, que de remuer le soleil! (1869:9)

> What bliss it would be to climb up there beside her with his arm around her waist, listening to her voice and basking in the radiance of her eyes while her dress swept the yellow leaves along the ground! The boat could stop, and they had only to disembark; it was all so simple, yet budging the sun would have been an easier proposition. (1964:21)

Baldick uses about eight more words to both expand and compensate. He moves the conditional to the main clause of a complete sentence. He moves the exclamation mark since he is splitting the sentence. His choice of *bliss* for *bonheur* ('happiness') signals the potential physicality of the feeling. His expansion follows Flaubert's lead, so that each description of a couple walking could be read as an erotic embrace. We might wonder why Baldick was not content to say 'yet it would have been easier to move the sun'.

Although it is difficult to imagine Frédéric leading a useful life anywhere, Paris does seem to elicit especially irresistible impulses of debauchery and dilettantism. After an orgiastic masked-ball in the first chapter of Part II his dream consciousness brings together prophetically (after all, this is a novel) images of the women who act on his senses:

> Un autre soif lui était venue, celle des femmes, du luxe et de tout ce que comporte l'existence parisienne. Il se sentait quelque peu

étourdi, comme un homme qui descend d'un vaisseau; et, dans l'hallucination du premier sommeil, il voyait passer et repasser continuellement les épaules de la Poissarde, les reins de la Débardeuse, les mollets de la Polonaise, la chevelure de la Sauvagesse. Puis deux grands yeux noirs, qui n'étaient pas dans le bal, parurent; et légers comme des papillons, ardents comme des torches, ils allaient, venaient, vibraient, montaient dans la corniche, descendaient jusqu'à sa bouche. Frédéric s'acharnait à reconnaître ces yeux sans y parvenir. Mais déjà le rêve l'avait pris; il lui semblait qu'il était attelé près d'Arnoux, au timon d'un fiacre, et que la Maréchale, à califourchon sur lui, l'éventrait avec ses éperons d'or. (1869:128-129)

Another thirst had come upon him: the thirst for women, for luxury, for everything life in Paris implies. He felt slightly dazed, like a man disembarking from a ship; and in the hallucination of his first sleep he saw passing to and from before him the Fishwife's shoulders, the Stevedore's back, the Polish girl's calves, and the Savage Woman's hair. Then two big dark eyes, which were not at the ball, appeared; and, light as butterflies, bright as torches, they darted here and there, quivered, flew up to the ceiling, then swooped down to his lips. Frédéric struggled to recognize these eyes without success. But already a dream had taken hold of him; he thought he was harnessed side by side with Arnoux in the shafts of a cab, and the Marshal, sitting astride him, was tearing his belly open with her golden spurs. (1964:133-134)

Although the comparable effects overall may vary when read out of context (which situates the women wearing these costumes), this is close to flawless. It adds to the surface movement: *allaient, venaient* becomes *darted here and there*; *descendait jusqu'à* becomes *swooped down to*; *vibraient* adds the notion of *quivered*; *l'eventrait* is unpacked as *tearing his belly open*.

As Part II comes to a close, Frédéric believes he can profit from Madame Arnoux's exasperation with her husband's infidelities. She was in the prime of what the French call a woman's second youth:

D'ailleurs, elle touchait au mois d'août des femmes, époque tout à la fois de réflexion et de tendresse, où la maturité qui commence colore le regard d'une flamme plus profonde, quand la force du coeur se mêle à l'expérience de la vie, et que, sur la fin de

ses épanouissements, l'être complet déborde de richesses dans
l'harmonie de sa beauté. (1869:273)

Besides, she was approaching the August of a woman's life, a period which combined reflection and tenderness, when the maturity
which is beginning kindles a warmer flame in the eyes, when strength
of heart mingles with experience of life, and when, in the fullness
of its development, the whole being overflows with a wealth of harmony and beauty. (1964:272)

This is another typical instance of Baldick's adroit rearranging: strengthening the opening metaphor by omission of 'the month of'; expanding an
appositional phrase into a clause. Gender gives him some trouble. The 'whole
being' (*l'être complet*) is masculine, but Madame Arnoux is the person
being discussed – it is not a question of the August of a man's life. This
means that *ses épanouissements* – clearly referring to women in their second youth with Madame Arnoux as their exemplar – when rendered as *its
development* has the English reader referring back to *life* (or possibly *experience, heart* or *strength*), not, however, to Madame Arnoux. Perhaps a
little more interpretation would have helped, for example: 'when nearing
the end of her blooming, a woman's whole being overflows with gifts of
harmonious beauty'.

In Flaubert's interlacing of the political and the social, Louis-
Philippe's abdication coincides with the sore-throat complications of
Madame Arnoux's son. This conjunction makes Frédéric and Madame
Arnoux's assignation inconceivable in retrospect. Frédéric, out of spite,
begins his liaison with her husband's official mistress Rosanette.

Flaubert's language is so spare in the one instance where he arouses
readers' unforced compassion that Baldick achieves a nearly semantically
isomorphic translation and an equally moving passage. This is at the close
of the second chapter of Part III where Louise Roque, the young heiress
from his home town, discovers she had been at most a convenient diver-
sion. She and her maid go through the 1848 barricades to Frédéric's
apartment:

  Enfin, elles arrivèrent chez Frédéric. Louise tira la sonnette avec
  vigueur, plusieurs fois. La porte s'entre-bâilla et le concierge répon-
  dit à sa demande:
  – «Non!»
  – «Mais il doit être couché?»

– «Je vous dis que non! Voilà près de trois mois qu'il ne couche pas chez lui!»

Et le petit carreau de la loge retomba nettement comme une guillotine. Elles restaient dans l'obscurité, sous la voûte. Une voix furieuse leur cria:

– «Sortez donc!»

La porte se rouvrit; elles sortirent.

Louise fut obligée de s'asseoir sur une borne; et elle pleura, la tête dans ses mains, abondamment, de tout son coeur. Le jour se levait, des charrettes passaient. (354-5)

At last they arrived at Frédéric's house. Louise pulled the bell vigorously several times. The door opened a little way, and in response to her inquiry the concierge answered:

'No!'

'But he must be in bed?'

'I tell you, no! He hasn't slept at home for nearly three months now!'

And the little window of the lodge dropped into place like a guillotine. They stood there in the darkness, under the archway. A furious voice shouted at them:

'Get out!'

The door opened again; they went out.

Louise was obliged to sit down on a gate-stone; and with her head in her hands, she wept copiously, from the bottom of her heart. Day was breaking; some carts went by. (1964:349)

Part III, another authorial *tour de force*, balances and weaves together the collapse of the Second Republic, the death of Frédéric and Rosanette's little boy, the embittering ending of his engagement to a wealthy widow, Louise's marriage to his 'best friend' Deslauriers, and the bayonetting of one of his friends by another. In the penultimate chapter, sixteen years later (veritably the time of Flaubert's writing the novel) Madame Arnoux visits him. Afraid that she has come to make up for the rendezvous missed the day of Louis-Philippe's abdication, Frédéric rolls a cigarette. As she gets up to leave, she gives him a maternal blessing:

Et elle le baisa au front comme une mère.

Mais elle parut chercher quelque chose, et lui demanda des ciseaux.

Elle défit son peigne; tous ses cheveux blancs tombèrent.

Elle s'en coupa, brutalement, à la racine, une longue mèche.
— «Gardez-les! adieu!»
Quand elle fut sortie, Fédéric ouvrit sa fenêtre, Madame
Arnoux, sur le troittoir, fit signe d'avancer à un fiacre qui passait.
Elle monta dedans. La voiture disparut.
Et ce fut tout. (1869:424)

And she kissed him on the forehead like a mother.
[At this point Baldick does some discreet rewriting:]
But she seemed to be looking for something, and finally
[adverb inserted] she asked him for some scissors.
She took out her comb, and all her white hair fell over her
shoulders [prepositional phrase added].

Baldick tones down the reader's shock at her self-immolating gesture (and
removes pre- Freudian overtones). He could have written 'She cut some off
[the reflexive makes action harsher], brutally, at the root, a long lock'.
Instead, he writes:

With an abrupt gesture [action classified] she cut off a long lock
close to her head.
'Keep it. Good-bye!'
When she had gone out, Frédéric opened his window. On the pave-
ment Madame Arnoux beckoned to a passing cab. She got in. The
carriage disappeared.
And that was all. (415-6)

The novel, however, is not quite over. Frédéric and Deslauriers resume
their friendship and also resume the narrative we have just read:

Et ils résumèrent leur vie.
Ils l'avaient manquée tous les deux, celui qui avait rêvé l'amour,
celui qui avait rêvé le pouvoir. Quelle en était la raison?
— «C'est peut-être le défaut de la ligne droite», a dit Frédéric.
— «Pour toi, cela se peut. Moi, au contraire, j'ai péché par
excès de rectitude, sans tenir compte de mille choses secon-
daires, plus fortes que tout. J'avais trop de logique, et toi de
sentiment.»
Puis, ils accusèrent le hasard, les circonstances, l'époque où ils
étaient nés. (1869:426-7)

Baldick subtly interprets, toning down; their lives were not really tragic:

> And they looked back over their lives. [Instead of 'summed up' which suggests not only the itemization that they have just completed but a judgment that they proceed to invoke.]
> They had both failed [more literally and accurately 'they had missed out on life'], one to realize his dreams of love, the other to fulfil his dreams of power. What was the reason?
> 'Perhaps it's because we didn't steer a straight course,' said Frédéric.
> 'That may be true in your case. But I, on the contrary, was far too rigid in my line of conduct, and I failed to take into account a thousand-and-one minor factors which were really all-important. I was too logical, while you were too sentimental.' [Baldick gives Deslauriers far more lexical fluency.]
> Then they blamed chance, circumstances, the times into which they were born. (1964:417-8)

This may be English interference, but *accused* sounds stronger than *blamed*. Still, Baldick's every emendation adds to authentic characterization.

Flaubert ends the novel on this reminiscence, a truncated visit to the local brothel, subtly interpreted by the substitution of 'happiest time' for *de meilleur* ('the best we had'):

> – «C'est là ce que nous avons eu de meilleur!» dit Frédéric.
> – «Oui, peut-être bien? c'est là ce que nous avons eu de meilleur!» dit Deslauriers. (1869:428)

> 'That was the happiest time we ever had,' said Frédéric.
> 'Yes, perhaps you're right. That was the happiest time we ever had,' said Deslauriers. (1964:419)

The two well-known novels we have looked at are admittedly long, and their highly competent, often inspired, translators have helped keep them in the canon. The novels have a standing in world literature that could not have been accomplished without translation.

Yet, as a genre, the novel is not dependent upon language alone. That is, some 'badly written' novels like Theodore Dreiser's *Sister Carrie* or Madame de Staël's *Corinne* read just as well or better in translation. Readers of a writer's own literature are often amazed by a writer's standing elsewhere. Poe, whom we looked at earlier, is an American writer, but it could more accurately be said that he belongs to comparative literature rather than to American literature.

The final test case returns us to Baudelaire, this time to a work of his for which there is no translation in print: *La Fanfarlo* (1847, 1869). Greg Boyd translated it for a small press in 1986, but his translation can only be found in libraries that recognized the urgency of purchase when it came out. The examples that follow come from an unpublished translation (copyright 1996) by Carmen Swoffer-Pena, a young American Francophile, who translated the novelette both to study Baudelaire's irony and to oblige fellow doctoral students whose French was not up to Baudelaire's lexicon. In this captivatingly ironic novelette Baudelaire models the vivacious 'other woman', the title character, on the Spanish dancer Lola Montès; the triumphant wife Madame de Cosmelly on his own sister-in-law (married to his stepbrother from his father's first marriage), and the duped poet-theatre critic Samuel Cramer on himself. As for Monsieur de Cosmelly, he is simply a trophy spouse.

A key untranslatable word in Baudelaire's language, we remember, is *volupté*. Like Scott Moncrieff in *The Charterhouse of Parma*, Swoffer-Pena tries to avoid using it. While I would dispute this translation strategy, it is one that expands the text for a bilingual reader or a teacher of literature in translation. The interliminal space, we might note, acts like an analogue of the perfumes in 'Correspondances' (1857), probably Baudelaire's best known poem: 'Ayant l'expansion des choses infinies' ('having the expansion of infinite things'). To round out our discussion, let us simply look at the way Baudelaire uses *volupté* and how Swoffer-Pena finesses it. The fact that the word has come into academic English as 'a pleasurable, physically reactive feeling or response of erotic implications' has not made her task as a translator easier. Basically, in this novelette, *volupté* is a question of over-wrought cuisine and chi-chi boudoir decor.

A good chef should be constrained by 'une loi particulière et voluptuaire à connaître les propriétés chimiques des matières'. In this way for a 'fête amoureuse' they could put together 'des éléments presque inflammables, prompts à parcourir le système organique, comme l'acide prussique, à se volatiliser comme l'éther' (*Fanfarlo* 1976:575). Swoffer-Pena reminds us that here the taste buds and the digestive system are at stake:

67

a particular, sensual law, to be familiar with the chemical properties of matter, and know how to discover, if necessary, for special cases like for example, a love feast, some culinary elements which are almost inflammable, ready to travel through the organic system like prussic acid, and finally [adverb inserted to suggest some duration] to volatize like ether. (1996)

An appropriately outfitted boudoir would be a 'ravissant taudis, qui tenait à la fois du mauvais lieu et du sanctuaire'. On the walls would be seen suggestive paintings 'pleines d'une voluptés espagnoles: des chairs très blanches sur des fonds très noirs' (1976:576). Swoffer-Pena believes the key here is a visually induced stimulated sense of touch: this 'ravishing hovel, which was simultaneously an evil place and a sanctuary... some sensual Spanish paintings; very white flesh on very black backgrounds'.

However, in the moral that Baudelaire sometimes seems to imply, almost in spite of himself, these satiated pleasures, these simulated, artifice-provoked desires cannot bring about *volupté à deux*, let alone *jouissance* ('sexual ecstasy') as experienced by women. No, and here the fatality of these states of experience comes to the foreground: they are solipsistic experiences, and in the opinion of Baudelaire's narrator, they are chiefly male prerogatives. Baudelaire says of Samuel:

> Du reste, comme il arrive aux hommes exceptionnels, il était souvent seul dans son paradis, nul ne pouvant l'habiter avec lui; et si, de hasard, il l'y ravissait et l'y traînait presque de force, elle restait toujours en arrière: ainsi dans le ciel où il régnait, son amour commençait d'être triste et malade de la mélancolie du bleu, comme un royal solitaire' (1976:578).

Swoffer-Pena is no more sympathetic:

> Besides, as happens with exceptional men, he was often alone in his paradise. No one was capable of occupying it with him. And, if, by chance, he took her and dragged her there almost by force, she was always behind. Therefore, in the heavens where he reigned, his love was beginning to be sad and he, like a lonely prince was becoming sick from the melancholia of the blue. (1996)

The French may sound beautiful, but the English with its somewhat more monologic rhythm reminds us of the inherent inequality of this relationship. What we sense in the interliminal cannot be neutralized by the writer's wit.

68

The interliminal expands when we recognize that it uses recurring words of disturbing ambivalence in Baudelaire's work. It is no wonder that prose poem 18 'L'Invitation au Voyage' in *Le Spleen de Paris* (1862, 1869) keeps *luxe* ('luxuriousness'), *ordre* ('order'), and *beauté* ('beauty') – along with a highly spiced cuisine and fabulous antiques and horticulture of the poem of the same name, with which we opened our discussion of Stendhal. The *volupté* of the poem has been omitted. It is the poet's *pensées* ('thoughts') that *dorment* ('slumber') or *roulent* ('tumble') on the breast of the woman being addressed. She is his *tulipe noire*, his *dahlia bleu*, if set in a frame, she could coincide with her own analogy, her proper *correspondance*.

Was what we just now cited as a seemingly male prerogative for Baudelaire's narrator in *La Fanfarlo*, a male problem in fact, or a problem for humankind? It is *translation and the interliminal space* that makes readers even notice gender and consider it an issue. In the penultimate paragraph of this prose poem Baudelaire pronounces in a tone we re-construct as solemn:

> Chaque homme porte en lui sa dose d'opium naturel, incessam-ment sécrétée et renouvelée, et, de la naissance à la mort, combien comptons-nous d'heures remplies par la jouissance positive, par l'action réussi et décidée? Vivrons-nous jamais, passerons-nous jamais dans ce tableau qu'a peint mon esprit, ce tableau qui te ressemble? (1976:303)

To translate as we would have done automatically a quarter century ago:

> Each man bears within himself his dose of natural opium, con-stantly secreted and renewed, and from birth to death, how many hours filled with positive *jouissance*, with successful, decisive action can we count?

I kept *jouissance* because it has been in English since the 1550s as both 'use' (as of 'profit, use of an asset') and as 'enjoyment'. Further, the poet is addressing a woman toward whom he feels affectionate, albeit not passionate, so a word with erotic connotations is not amiss. In my read-ing, admittedly biased by my notion of Baudelaire's relationship to women, this judgment is reserved for men.

However, Edward K. Kaplan's 1989 translation, which received the

Lewis Galantière Prize of the American Translators Association, gives
Baudelaire the benefit of a larger view, bringing men and women into the
equality of human frailty:

> Each of us carries within a dose of natural opium, ceaselessly
> secreted and renewed, and, from birth to death,

Once Kaplan had made this choice, he had to reject *jouissance* for a more
common word:

> how many hours can we count filled with concrete delight, with
> well-executed and resolute action? Will we ever live, will we ever
> enter that picture painted by my mind, that painting which resem-
> bles you? (1989:39)

Kaplan has thus effectively enlarged the circumference. We may dispute
his boundary (I do), but without the translation we might never have real-
ized it could be read inclusively.

8. Conclusion: The Text and Translation Equation

Our discussion has been leading to a pronouncement, one which should come as no surprise: in literary criticism there should be potentially equal standing for original texts and their translations. Granting equal standing to the text of the original and the text(s) of the translation is not the same as according them equal merit. Nor is it getting deeply involved in the unsolvable concept of equivalence (which everyone can understand and no one can explain). Equal standing here means that we are dealing with literary equations. We need texts on both sides of the equals sign – quite apart from any claims that may be made about formal or functional equivalence. Even canonical translations accorded consensus-merit like the King James Bible, the Schlegel-Tieck Shakespeare and the Urquhart-Motteux Rabelais have in no way deterred retranslations. Baudelaire's Poe and George's Baudelaire are already canonical. (It is likely that Scott Moncrieff's Proust and Baldick's Huysmans are on their way to becoming canonical, and their *Charterhouse of Parma* and *Sentimental Education* could become canonical by default.)

We have just seen three translation styles: the somewhat overwrought normalizing translation by Scott Moncrieff, the somewhat downplayed normalizing of Baldick, and the tempered neoliteralism of Swoffer-Penna. With respect to our terminology, Scott Moncrieff and Baldick were subtly domesticating, target-oriented and meaning-based. Swoffer-Penna, also subtle, was foreignizing, source-oriented and more language-based. It seems reasonable to assume that all three translators put themselves into the French texts and surveyed the scene as directed by the narrator. In each of the texts the narrator's irony allowed the translator also to maintain some distance for judgment.

However, regardless of the translators' critical strategies, their results all encourage, I would say, a comparable degree of collaboration on the part of stereoscopic readers. Hence all three guide us or challenge us with provisional boundaries for an interliminal space. We can explore and complete with the cues they have provided. These spaces, which change with even our own readings, add an aura, as well as an impact. Such reader collaboration will enrich reading long after the demise of the Postmodernism and the aesthetics of required collaboration.

A translation remains what the copyright law says: a derivative work.

But it is a derivative that validates the etymology. It is, as Benjamin's translator Harry Zohn put it so well, the work's 'afterlife'. Works of the past are neither recovered nor recuperated in their first language unless translated. Take, for example, the renewed readership of popular nineteenth-century women writers like Madame de Staël, George Sand or Louise Colet; this readership stems from translation into English. Some works have been re-translated with every major fluctuation of the rhythms of cultural history. They have stayed alive for successive generations. The resuscitation of others, untranslated for decades, even centuries, seems to have burst through a time warp.

Madame de Staël provides a ready example. Her *Corinne* (1807) was translated into English in 1807, 1833 and 1889. The 1833 translation by Isabel Hill and Letitia E. Landon went through thirty-two editions between 1833 and 1933. It was in harmony first with Victorian taste and later for those with Victorian taste. For late-twentieth-century women's studies, we needed Avriel Goldberger's 1987 retranslation (see my 1987 text description).

More tellingly, de Staël had written clairvoyant prose pieces, relevant for post-colonial and cultural studies. These were ignored until 1994, when de Staël's prose pieces on slavery were translated by Françoise Massardier-Kenney, Dorish Kadish and Sharon Bell in *Translating Slavery*. The translators avoid anachronisms. Still, we have inescapably contemporary diction expressing views, not unkind but considerably more patronizing than we would expect from a de Staël were she living today. The translators have admitted to making her remarks as inoffensive as possible. This does not mean that they have changed de Staël's sentiments, but it means that when confronted by a term, they chose the least offensive option. Although I do not want to confuse the issue of equal standing, it is simply a fact that de Staël's translators took more pains with editing than she did with re-writing. Anyone who has taught this material knows that the translators had to make decisions on antecedence and misplaced modifiers.

The pronouncement of equal standing reconciles what we noticed earlier with cultural history and literary criticism which, in my opinion, determine translation theory at any given moment. (As we mentioned earlier, current literary criticism and continental philosophy have taken over Benjamin, starting with his essays on translation and language.)

That 'any given' moment in the heartbeat metaphor of cultural history in Chapter 4 will determine how we read literature, how some of us will read literature we know to be translated literature, and, above all, how we will assess the value of what we have read. The theoretical observation I have developed and demonstrated is that literary texts are fuller when read with their translations, regardless of whether literature and literary norms are in an expansive or restrictive phase. This is because taken together these texts and translations loosely enclose an interliminal space of meaning, allusion and sound. This space will vary from reader to reader; for an individual reader from one reading time to the next; and most markedly from one period to another. This last variance may well elicit a new translation because changing norms in culture and, consequently, rhetoric have brought too many disjunctions into that space. (We might wonder whether Scott Moncrieff's *The Charterhouse of Parma*, examined in the last chapter, would begin to sound like a Bulwer Lytton pastiche within another decade or two.) What sounded normal to earlier readers, what called up associations that seemed to fit, may begin to sound silly or quaint, overdone or inappropriate.

Whatever our assessment of the translation in question, whether cultural consensus is expanding or contracting, reading literature with a translation will always ensure our collaboration with the author, and it will always add more to our experience of the work. A critical reading of literature entails a theoretical – analytical – approach to translation.

Afterword

To Contemplators ... to Cavillers

Returning to the 'future' with which we began, *L'Eve future* and the *rêveurs* and *railleurs* to which that novel was dedicated, let us reconsider appropriate translations as we anticipate objections to the ensuing demonstration. I should prefer to forestall as many objections as I can, for in human sociality words once said cannot be unsaid. (The loss of many literary works through time, a fact I referred to in Chapter 2, may well have often resulted from the effects of effable words with ineffable results.) Our turn-of-the-century fixation on memory in research and discussion throughout the arts and sciences and our daily confrontation with the residue and repetition of tragic political events – all of this is a reminder that words can do as much damage as sticks and stones.

To those who have taken the time to apply the strategy of systematic stereoscopic reading to their preferred authors and literatures, thank you for taking on contemplation. (Perhaps like the title character in Molière's *Bourgeois Gentilhomme* you have been doing stereoscopic reading since you began either to teach or translate.) To those who found the discussion too peripheral or irrelevant to bother with, my apologies; you really should have stopped early on, instead of sticking around to cavil. *Caviller* can easily modulate into *cavalier*.

As for myself, I have come across something rewarding in every study of translation I have ever read, even when, perhaps especially when, I privately disagree.

One stricture it behooves us all to remember: to read books first as their authors wrote them, before we bemoan the absence of the books we wish they had written instead.

> The preceding monograph was on translation and literary criticism.
> Period.

In the case of this essay it will be noted that I deliberately avoided examples that would bring in complicating issues. I did not want us distracted from an examination of the interliminal *per se*, but, aware that it could not be done in a vacuum, I chose the most neutral examples from the Western canon available to me from my own teaching and research experience (including descriptive translation studies).

Therefore, I avoided by design

- implications of patronage whether by overt censorship or by the marketplace;
- effects of overt unequal political relations despite my inherited guilt as a) a citizen of a world power, b) a member of an oppressive race, and c) an accidental speaker of a widely disseminated language; and
- applications for those who will make their living doing non-literary translation. (I shall get to these in the Appendix on pedagogy.)

I mentioned only in passing

- unequal power relations of gender. I not only feel qualified to deal with them, I most emphatically do deal with them on a daily basis. Vis-à-vis translation I have done so in print elsewhere on many an occasion.

All of the foregoing are worth a book of their own. All already have a place in this series. Many such books have been published, and thanks to the convergence of translation and cultural studies many more are sure to come.

It should be evident that my espousal of foreignizing translation, which I renamed 'neoliteralism' at the American Translators Association conference in October 1993, and my advocacy of stereoscopic reading are proofs that I prefer translations that correct the deformations caused by unequal power relations. Further, we will not be cognizant of the inequality unless we sight the gap between the boundaries of text and translation, until we explore the interliminal.

What I have done has been to show how translating and translations make the reading of literary texts richer. 'Richer' includes more complex, more problematic, more troublesome.

If I were to embark on a crusade in the future, it would have two thrusts: in terms of translation standards, I would exhort translators to be sensitive to changing norms. In terms of conceptualizing translation, I would exhort students of translation at whatever stage in their careers to be receptive to everything about them, especially to ideas that disturb their preconceptions. Do not worry, I would preach, about being wrong or making a mistake. There is plain common sense to handle egregious errors, and even errors, as the linguists among us have pointed out, can be meaningful. That would comprise my crusade for the *future*. But, to recapitulate, this monograph is only the *Eve*.

Appendix on Pedagogy: The *Ennui* Factor

Ennui, incidentally, is a word that English speakers borrowed shortly before Baudelaire gave it currency, but one that is not recorded in American usage until 1857, the year of *Les Fleurs du mal*. Whatever and wherever caused the usage ricochet, *ennui* is for the teaching profession a consummation devoutly to be thwarted. Those who teach skills and facts often seem particularly vulnerable. (That is, how can they stay interested in going through the same material year after year? After a while, even the students may start looking the same to them.) When a teacher is bored or burned out, there is almost automatically a bad learning environment. Students typically react unproductively to routinized instruction and faked enthusiasm. It is certainly fortunate and probably true that prospective translators are so enthusiastic about learning that they will personally compensate for a teacher's *ennui*, but we should not count on it.

(There are two basic assumptions here: first, that you believe what you teach is something someone else will be better off learning; second, that you have the presence to put this something across to someone else.)

The first rule of successful teaching has to be put negatively: Make sure you are not bored. Boredom-avoidance strategies may ultimately be personal and idiosyncratic. But to state the obvious for the record, one preventive panacea is to stay in a learning mode, or to borrow a term from Karate, to keep a beginner's mind.

This is the basic reason why the study of translation is so exhilarating: you are constantly learning new things and constantly challenged to bring the new data, the new ideas into your teaching repertory. Studying translation involves strategies that, as demonstrated in the accompanying monograph, enrich the reading of literature. Those strategies are vital for inculcating the techniques of textual analysis that go into translator training.

There is a corollary to the first rule: To keep learning you must keep changing, either your material or your manner. If you find yourself resisting change, attracted by routine, you are manifesting the first symptoms of *ennui*.

One comforting reinforcement for change, more like a natural law than a rule: Each class — each group of students gathered together as a class — has its own dynamic and this requires a special response on your part. Even when you are in a situation where you are obliged to keep the same syllabus, you will not have the same class and cannot teach it the same way.

These rules undergird the teaching categories below. All based on postsecondary education in the United States, these categories show how translation skills, sometimes stereoscopic reading in its baldest form, are used across the curriculum.

Languages Across the Curriculum

Known both as LAC and LxC, this is a movement in the United States and English-speaking Canada closely related to content-based language instruction. (I shall leave aside the Canadian strategies that are a response to the Canadian bilingual language policy, except to note that they inspired the movement in the United States). It has been my privilege to serve as Associate Director for training, including proficiency testing, under my colleague H. Stephen Straight, the psycholinguist who is one of the U.S. leaders in the movement. There are several models in use. For example, a course can be taught in the language that dominates the subject, for example, Renaissance art taught in Italian. Or if that is impractical, such a course could be team-taught; with a faculty member from art history and one from Italian dividing the class sessions. (As may be imagined, there are several effective submodels for this.) Or there can be language instruction that is geared to a field from the beginning, like German for engineers.

On my own campus we use international graduate students to lead study groups in the languages appropriate to the field; for example, international business and immigration history routinely have two to seven language study groups in three to five different languages.

A demonstration of what goes on in a language study group in international business would be in fact a 'translation' of what was demonstrated in comparing Baudelaire's translations of Poe in Chapter 5 or George's of Baudelaire in Chapter 6. Only much more focused. These students working toward a Masters in Business Administration are intent on identifying the information that is implicit, the cultural biases that lurk in the interliminal, absences in the text that native readers supply. I might add that this weekly group-study enables them to maintain their language proficiency and enlarge their field-specific vocabulary.

Elsewhere in our curriculum, we evangelize for stereoscopic reading. (For students and faculty stymied by research in a language they cannot handle personally, there is the University Translation Referral Service, founded in 1973.)

Comparative and General Literature

By comparative and general literature I mean courses in which literature in translation can be taught along with English-language literature.

For the sake of parsimony, let me just say that such undergraduate courses (courses that fulfil requirements for a bachelor's degree), in part because of LxC staff evangelizing and encouragement, are much more likely to accommodate foreign-language texts now than they were a few years ago. (On our campus, 1991 was the watershed date.)

Let me move to graduate seminars where it might be imagined that I spend all class time perched on a boundary to squint into an interliminal abyss. By no means! A seminar is a near-peer experience, and the students are like so many team players with the instructor as a combination captain-coach. What was seen in Chapters 5, 6 and 7 was similar to what might be my own contribution during a session.

But a few explanatory reminders about American graduate education are probably in order. By 'graduate' is meant European 'postgraduate'. (Readers are aware that transcripts evaluation is a matter for admissions specialists, regardless of who is going where. Notarized translations of the transcripts may be the only common worldwide requirement. A decade ago I became a New York State Notary Public to facilitate work in the Referral Service mentioned above.) The United States requires a certain number of postgraduate courses prior to comprehensive written and oral examinations at both master's and doctoral levels (eight or nine courses for a master's, ten to twelve for a doctorate). To be admitted to candidacy means that students have completed coursework and examinations, including research-language proficiencies, and have had their dissertation prospectus accepted. They have five years in which to write their dissertation. A majority of master's students expect to go on for their doctorate, and doctoral students, almost without exception, are preparing for the professorate.

Thus, in such a seminar I have the responsibility of setting up an interactive environment in which my future colleagues and replacements can join me in pursuing a topic of mutual interest. In my case, all the authors cited in the preceding monograph have furnished topics. (What has been atypical for the examples just cited is the paucity of women writers, feminist readings and genetic criticism, which are as much features of my approach as stereoscopic reading.)

What mandates stereoscopic reading and attention to neoliteralism is a fact of enrolment specific to our own campus: my students come from the departments of art history, comparative literature, English and creative writing, and philosophy; very rarely from foreign languages where there is no doctoral programme and where the chief graduate interest is in language teaching. In a seminar, say, on Baudelaire, everyone will have access to a bilingual edition of *Les Fleurs du mal*, and most will need one. (I discourage their all using the same translation.) Some, however, will have invested only in a French edition.

Inevitably the discussion, including reports and seminar papers, involves descriptive translation studies and translation criticism that discriminates among translations. Indeed, in a seminar of fifteen there will be three or four students who prepare their own portfolio of translations and dialogic original poetry in addition to more traditional research papers.

How much translating qua translating goes on and how much descriptive translation analysis is involved depends on the seminar topic and the students enrolled. Inasmuch as all of my colleagues in comparative literature and many of my colleagues in English and creative writing and philosophy are published translators, I believe I am not atypical.

Literary and Non-Literary Translation Workshops

Nor are translation workshop atypical workshops. They are very much like creative-writing and play-writing workshops. Every participant is a translator, and every participant is a critic and editor. The prerequisites for our workshop complement, which was founded over a quarter of a century ago, are as follows: fluency in a source language (preferably not English), effective expression in a target language (usually English), a positive approach to painstaking textual problem-solving. A high degree of computer literacy is assumed. There is a team of instructors.

In the *literary workshop* a publishable piece of reasonable volume is expected by the end of the 14-week semester. The students choose their text in consultation with their tutor and other consultants. Most students are from comparative literature and creative writing. They are quite sensitive to the issues in cultural studies.

During most of the term the students enrolled in the literary workshop work one-on-one with the member of the instructional team most appropriate to their project. From time to time they meet with the non-literary workshop. At the end of each semester they present a recital, and they are eligible to submit their work to the anthology issue of a joint publication with creative-writing graduate students.

The literary workshop is demonstrably more efficient when it is organized as just indicated. Since 1971 other formats have been tried, but a format that requires weekly tutorials at the mutual convenience of instructor and students produces more high-quality work and, hence, more learner satisfaction. The norms are covert and have changed over the past quarter of a century as taste has changed. Since most students choose serious literature, there has been a discernible move toward neoliteral translations. Both tutor and tutee learn from the exchange.

The organization of the *non-literary workshop* varies from semester to semester depending on the students enrolled. The students come from a greater variety of disciplines than the literary workshop. This past semester they came from foreign language departments (Arabic, French, German, Hebrew, Italian, Japanese, Russian and Spanish), political science, sociology, philosophy and professional education. Sometimes the students are separated by language pair or direction. In the semester just past there were three subgroups: English to Spanish, German to English, and French and Spanish to English. The syllabus has a generalist orientation, making sure that subjects typically requiring translation are covered. Each brief (or assignment) requires lexical researching, and each brief is handed in twice: first for class criticism and then in a portfolio totalling 10,500 to 12,000 words. This is the group that does abstracts, minutes, vital documents and news analyses. Briefs are almost never repeated from one term to the next.

The non-literary workshop has an extremely entertaining and informative semi-weekly programme, predictably more fun in the conventional sense, than any of the other classes mentioned. Everyone learns a lot since the instructors put together a syllabus of topics they themselves want to learn more about. One sacred rule: instructors can make jokes about one another's mistakes; but they must always be kind and supportive to students. (Students can make jokes about instructors' mistakes; in over a quarter of a century we have never had students be anything but supportive with one another.)

Standards could be called normative; they certainly can be called conventional because we are training students to be responsive to how something is said and to use their ingenuity in finding an acceptable way to say what the source-sender intends the target-receiver to learn. A brief, the instructional team is agreed, can take from twenty minutes to infinity to complete. But at some point it must be turned in and take the evaluation consequences.

[If United States State Department proficiency codes are meaningful in this context, we might say our briefs require a source-language reading proficiency of 3 (understanding shared information among educated readers). In the target language writing proficiency translators should manifest a 5 (writing as and for educated native professionals).]

Returning to the *Ennui* Factor: A Final Manifesto

Clearly, boredom is rare in the classes just described. We want our students to encounter different approaches, even succumb to them. We have had as guest professors colleagues whose approaches differ markedly from what was stated in the body of this monograph: Itamar Even-Zohar, André Lefevere, Albrecht Neubert, Heidemarie Salevsky, Gideon Toury. (Three of our dissertations in comparative literature followed Even-Zohar.) Among the instructors on the team, we are definitely not of one mind: two philologists, a psycholinguist, a foreign-language pedagogue, an acoustical phonologist, a deconstructionist, and a secular eclectic who frequents continental philosophers (myself). This variety prevents boredom, and our mutual respect preserves open discussion.

Mutual respect and open discussion do not result from personality genes but from determined, non-Sartrean goodwill and a conviction that genuine collegiality provides a better learning environment.

Speaking for myself, I could not do without descriptive translation studies, but I could not limit myself to them, for I see them as a means, not an end. They perform for translation studies the function that concordances perform for national literature studies. They give us data. Then on the basis of such language evidence we can make informed assumptions about economic, political and moralistic forces operating in cultures through time, across social classes and among countries.

But the challenge to the brain comes after the patient data-collecting. Then the brain can be catapulted into the extrapolations and speculations the data suggests.

Nor could I do without non-literary translation. It is norm-ridden, tied to the status quo even while recording the changes taking place in the status quo. But there can be no complacency regarding the status quo. Too much attention to it can mask the changes or act as if there were none. (If proof is needed for that assertion, just look at any copy of the Chilean *La Nación* as the Pinochet regime was crumbling.) In the long run I find literature more clairvoyant.

Throughout the preceding monograph I was implicitly recommending keeping the boundaries sighted and the interliminal gap surveyed. But the clairvoyance of literature brings our interliminal linking of geopolitics and semantic space to an analogy with time and history. For my students and myself I recommend trying to stay on the hither side of the time lag. Literature, both serious and popular, offers the richest purview and preview.

As a translator, Baudelaire's intuitions about Poe have been verified by literary historians. Do his intuitions about Longfellow, a lesser poet than either, according to posterity, but a far better translator, show selective reading? As for us, we should remember that the Longfellow lines Baudelaire borrowed come from poems that work their way to energy and reconciliation: 'Hymn to the Night' and 'A Psalm of Life'. Or is *ennui* a pose of diffidence concealing enthusiasm? It had better be the latter for teachers involved in translation studies.

Translation lets us look back while we move ahead. In *reverie* and *raillery*.

Glossary

Translators need not only be aware of the generally accepted dictionary meanings. In literary translation they must also respect an author's idiosyncratic meanings and special coinages. Although they are expected to avoid anachronisms, they must simultaneously take into account what a word may have meant in an author's own era and culture (except in those rare instances where a pastiche is called for). At the same time they must remember that lexicographers are typically self-effacing scholars who see themselves as recording usage rather than legislating it.

The definitions that follow show how these expressions have been used in the preceding monograph. They are undoubtedly idiosyncratic and special also.

Afterlife: Benjamin's *Fortleben*, usually refers to the posterity of a work of literature after dissemination through translation. See pp. 10, 52, 72.

Alexandrine: A six-foot or 12-beat line of poetry. The foot is iambic (short/long). It is to French poetry what iambic pentameter is to English. See p. 43.

Aura: The ineffable affect of any work of art, that which emanates from it. Such an aura is sensed or felt but cannot be empirically described except by its effect upon viewers, listeners, readers, etc. A glorious translation like the Psalms in the King James Bible can have an aura that may be judged to have as much of an aura as the original from it derives. The aura may even be comparable, but it cannot be same. See p. 5.

Caesurae: Breaks (pauses) in a line of poetry. They are indicated both by the rhythm of the thought expressed and by punctuation.

Celtic Renaissance: The Irish literary revival from 1887, the date of W. B. Yeats's *The Wandering of Usheen* to his death in January 1939. See pp. 23, 25.

Comparative Literature: The discipline most receptive to translation studies in the United States. It has always been dependent on a forewarned use of translations since no one scholar could be expected to learn all the languages for even the most minimal list of world masterpieces. In the late 1960s it also became the most likely site for translator training, although this responsibility is frequently shared with creative writing. In most postsecondary institutions in the United States, the focus in comparative literature is on advanced degrees (MAs and PhDs). This means that proficiency in a language other than English is assumed, rather than taught. In the 1970s it was still said that European-school comparative literature compared literatures across national and linguistic boundaries, while American-school comparative literature also compared literature with other arts and disciplines. This was probably always an over-simplification. By the 1980s literary theory had come to be the purview of comparative literature, and this development increased the place of translation studies in the discipline.

Continental Philosophy: In the United States this term refers to phenomenological and existential philosophy. In the foregoing essay I have often used 'post-Heideggerian' interchangeably. It is opposed to analytic philosophy, which through its links with artificial intelligence and machine translation also nurtures translation studies, and parallel to American philosophy (Ralph Waldo Emerson, William James, Charles Santiago Peirce, John Dewey). However, in tandem with comparative literature it has mined Peircean semiotics and linguistics of every persuasion.

Conventions: Implicitly agreed upon standards or strategies, e.g. translating a French alexandrine into German or English iambic pentameter. See pp. 81-82.

Criticism: Evaluation and interpretation. An American comparatist or continental philosopher discussing *Kritik* should by convention say 'Critical Theory'.

Deconstruction: Hermeneutic criticism in its Postmodernist guise. Deconstructionists generally hope to be non-normative, and they feel free to be personal in their reactions. See p. 53.

Domesticating/Foreignizing: The polarities of translation style as coined by Lawrence Venuti (with some debt to Schleiermacher). A domesticating translation tries to make the translation sound as if written in the target language. A foreignizing translation tries to keep the foreign flavour.

Dynamic equivalence: The term used by Eugene A. Nida and Charles R. Taber in *Translation Theory and Practice* (Leiden: Brill, 1974). In a 1986 address to the American Translators Association, Nida changed the term to 'functional equivalence'. This change is not mentioned in the printed conference proceedings but is taken up in a book co-authored with Jan de Waard the same year: *From One Language to Another* (Nashville, TN: Thomas Nelson). See p. 9.

Equivalence: An impression that the meaning is much the same in both languages. Various empirical and semi-empirical strategies have been developed to give translators and their patrons some confidence that this state has been achieved. In the interests of complete transfer Eugene Nida advocated the 'kernel sentence' technique in which each unit of meaning was recast into as simple a declarative sentence as possible before recasting in a stylistically pleasing form (see Nida and Tabor, in Bibliography). The Summer Institute of Linguistics recommended checking every utterance for the meaning carried by the word, the syntax, the discourse and the situation (see Larson, in Bibliography). See also the essays by Albrecht Neubert and Gregory Shreve in *Translation Horizons* for the direction of such equivalence checklists. See p. 71.

Genetic Criticism: A form of biographical criticism that takes account of Freudian and post-Freudian psychology. For such critics early drafts of a work can be as significant as the end result. Robin Orr Bodkin, at the 1995 ATA meeting in Nashville, Tennessee, was among the first to point to the usefulness of using translation drafts in this way. See p. 52.

Interliminal: Coined by Stephen David Ross, American philosopher in what in the United States is called the continental or post-Heideggerian tradition. Homi K. Bhabha, cited in translation studies, uses 'liminal' in describing cultural colonization. See Bhabha's 'Articulating the Archaic' in Peter Collier (ed) *Literary Theory Today* (Ithaca: Cornell, 1990), 203-18; *The Locale of Culture* (New York: Routledge, 1994); *Displacements. Identities in Question,* ed. Angelika Bammer (Bloomington: Indiana, 1994). Sanford Budick and Wolfgang Iser call their conference proceedings *The Translatability of Cultures. Figurations of the Space Between* (Palo Alto: Stanford University, 1996). However, translation is used in their anthology for the most part in its broadest definitions. Klaus Reichert nevertheless discusses the Buber-Rosenzweig Bible (169-83) as "an attempt at colonizing the space in between two cultures" (181). He means here an invented language where Hebrew structures in German show German as a transformation of Hebrew. In their anthology *Between Languages and Cultures. Translation and Cross-Cultural Texts* (University of Pittsburgh, 1995) Anuradha Dingwaney and Carol Maier focus on translation as the site between languages and cultures. According to most of their collaborators, it is the site where harm occurs. For example, when a non-Western text is made to conform to Western expectations, at the very least its distinctive features may be smoothed or removed. They do not use interliminal as an area where meaning and style gain. See p. 7.

Modernism: Used here arbitrarily as a time and generation frame for arts that do not fit a traditional mould, from 1913, the New York Armory Art Exhibit, to 1948 when T. S. Eliot received the Nobel Prize for Literature. It is hard to characterize. I prefer its intellectual and restrained side, for example from Cézanne to Picasso to Mondrian or Mallarmé to Yeats and Valéry; Flaubert to Virginia Woolf and Proust. But Joyce, the American Lost Generation, Surrealists and Hispanic *Modernismo* also fit in this time period. See pp. 23, 28, 39.

Neoliteral: a term introduced at the American Translators Association meeting in Philadelphia, October 6-10, 1993 to cover translations which defer to the source text. In the terminology used in this volume such a strategy is thus language-based, source-oriented and foreignized. It is much the same as what used to be called a philological translation. 'Neoliteral' will cover any kind of text in which a Benjaminian echo can be heard; it is more inclusive than Venuti's 'foreignized', which is applied especially to major-power translations of postcolonial texts.

Norms: The conventions (in the sense of implicitly agreed upon standards) of acceptable rhetoric and content. See pp. 23, 53.

Persona: The character (or characters) the author assumes in order to tell the story.

Polysystem: Whether perspective, approach or strategy, the term was apparently first used by Itamar Even-Zohar, Tel-Aviv scholar, in the early

1970s. In over-simplified terms he was adapting the systems concept of Russian Formalism to analyze the historical development of Hebrew literature. By the mid-1970s the notion had been taken up by other scholars in Israel and by scholars in the Benelux countries. The polysystem perspective reminds us that any literature contains not only many traditional genres but many levels of literature, from sacred texts to soap operas. The literatures of Israel and the Benelux countries provided excellent examples inasmuch as they had been influenced by the successive literary norms of the literatures they imported both by study of foreign languages and by translation. Since much of Even-Zohar's work was in Hebrew, most graduate students, at least in North America, learned about the polysystem approach through Gideon Toury's *In Search of a Theory of Translation* (Tel Aviv: Porter Institute, 1980) and from selected essays by André Lefevere. Although Toury no longer promotes the term qua term but uses 'descriptive translation studies' instead, it still has currency. It has considerable appeal because it not only provides quantifiable data but also because it restricts the terrain of analysis. More attention is given to the target text than to the source text, and while Toury increasingly takes cognizance of what translators record of their own process in translating, what cannot be determined empirically is downplayed, when not rejected altogether. See pp. 9, 10, 82.

Postmodernism: A very broad ideological spectrum in the arts and sciences and society at large. Implied in the label is a disaffection with whatever belief system is held responsible for giving human beings, individually or collectively, a false sense of confidence in progress. Followers of Michel Foucault speak of a new episteme, i.e. what is considered certain knowledge. Followers of Thomas Kuhn speak instead of a new 'paradigm'. The 'new' episteme or paradigm is relativist and regards natural laws and political systems presumably built on natural laws as temporary conventions at best. See pp. 2, 23, 27.

Pseudotranslation: An original work, frequently a pastiche, put forward as a translation. See pp. 25, 26.

Source-oriented/Target-oriented: The polarities of the translation spectrum, i.e. using the source text as primary guide or using the audience as a guide.

Speculative Tradition: The tradition that gets its guidelines from speculative philosophy. Gregory Shreve (see *Translation Horizons*) classifies such studies as literary and academic, in any event, non-empirical. Those in the speculative tradition, by no means a school, are somewhat sceptical vis-à-vis the scientific method. They reason that translation is an activity impelled by human beings in social situations and thus dynamic in essence. The attitude of the researcher is an inevitable component of any data collected.

Stereoscopic Reading: A term coined by translator-educator Joanne Englebert at the 1989 meeting of the American Translators Association in Albuquerque, New Mexico. It means simply using both the original language text and one (or more) translations while reading and teaching. Stereoscopic reading makes it possible to intuit and reason out the interliminal. See pp. 2-80.

Symbolism/Decadence: As an organized French movement Symbolism/Decadence was very short-lived, roughly 1880-87; as a dominant mode, roughly from 1857, the date of Baudelaire's *Les Fleurs du mal*, to the outbreak of World War I in 1914. By that time its impulses were absorbed by Modernism. See pp. 1, 28, 39, 52.

Bibliographical References

A translator would do well to follow the advice proferred in Henry James's *The American*: "Be a person on whom nothing is lost". This means almost any bit of information or insight may prove useful, as well as any book on any subject. Apart from that injunction, whether a translator should concentrate on translation studies *per se* or on the disciplines with which translation studies interacts is a matter of personal affinity. Just as there is a sense in which a translation is derivative, there is a sense in which books on translation studies *per se* are derivative. This bibliography will underscore my own preference for works that have affected my thinking about translation, rather than works about translation. It goes without saying that the works mentioned represent a personal choice. The list by no means includes all works I esteem highly and would recognize with grateful footnotes in more formal contexts than this series.

However, where literary criticism is the issue, both prospective and senior translation scholars need to be close to the vanguard, if not in it, keeping informed of the trends, even if reserving judgment on them. No matter how traditional our own personal rhetoric may be, no matter how bemused, say, a native speaker of English may be by some of the usages outside North America and the former British Commonwealth, it behooves translation scholars engaged in literary criticism to keep their normative allegiances in the background. For example, although I would never use coinages like 'translational' and 'translative', this does not mean I dismiss writers who do. On the contrary, I envy their creative aplomb. In the same vein I am leery of any system that either imposes, or relies on, normative allegiances. Communication, whether benevolent or malevolent, suggests that reasoned preservation of rhetorical conventions and belief systems is advantageous. Yet the dynamic of our speech-specific species makes change a constant. The works I have excluded should suggest that I eschew dogma and embrace tolerance.

My annotations address both beginning researchers and colleagues planning or revising advanced courses in comparative literature and translation studies.

Part One. Monograph Citations: these are the works cited

Literature Editions. The choice of illustrative works is personal and idiosyncratic, works I have lived with long enough to cite with some assurance. They are, as a result, unavoidably Western. They do illustrate one general stricture: it is imperative that translators always try to use the most authoritative editions. In comparing translations it is important to note what edition a translator used. Often a translation is an opportunity for revising the first-language text.

Bandy, W. R. (1971) *Seven Tales by Edgar Allen Poe with Their French Translations and a Prefatory Essay by Charles Baudelaire*, New York: Schocken Books.

Baudelaire, Charles (1976) *Œuvres complètes*, 2 vols, ed. Claude Pichois, Paris: Gallimard.

------ (1982) *Les Fleurs du mal*, trans. Richard Howard. Boston: David R. Godine.

------ (1986) *La Fanfarlo*, trans. Greg Boyd, Berkeley: Creative Arts Press. *'La Fanfarlo', which appeared in the first 1847 issue of the 'Bulletin de la Société des gens de lettres', was largely ignored, although it was published in Baudelaire's first 'Œuvres complètes' in 1869. Boyd's attractive bilingual edition is not listed in 'Books in Print'.*

------ (1989) *Parisian Prowler*, trans. Edward Kaplan, Athens: University of Georgia. *This is a translation of 'Le Spleen de Paris'. The prose poems were printed piecemeal in 1862 and took their final order in 1869.*

------ (1996) 'Fanfarlo', trans. Carmen Swoffer-Penna, unpublished typescript.

Beckett, Samuel (1957) *Endgame*, trans. by author. New York: Grove.

Camus, Albert (1942) *L'Étranger*, edited by Germaine Brée and Carlos Lynes Jr., New York: Appleton-Century-Crofts, 1955.

------ (1945) *The Stranger*, trans. Stuart Gilbert, New York: Random House, 1961; trans. Matthew Ward, New York: Alfred A. Knopf, 1988.

Chateaubriand, François-René de (1962) *Atala and René*, trans. Walter J. Cobb, New York: New American Library.

Flaubert, Gustave (1869) *L'Éducation sentimentale*, edited by P. M. Wetherill, Paris: Garnier Classique, 1984.

------ (1964) *Sentimental Education*, trans. Robert Baldick, London: Penguin.

Gates, David (1996) Review of two Beckett anthologies and Lois Gordon's Beckett biography, *New York Times Book Review* 26 (May):4.

George, Stefan (1891) *Die Blumen des Bösen*, Stuttgart: Klett-Cotta, 1983.

Goethe, Johann Wolfgang von (1774) *The Sufferings of Young Werther*, trans. Harry Steinhauer, dual-language, New York: Bantam, 1962.

Longfellow, Henry Wadsworth (1947) *Favorite Poems*, Garden City, New York: Doubleday.

Staël-Necker, Germaine de (1795) 'Mirza or Letters of a Traveller', trans. Françoise Massardier-Kenney in Doris Kadish and Françoise Massardier-Kenney (eds) *Translating Slavery: Gender & Race in French Women's Writing, 1783-1823*, Kent, Ohio: Kent State University Press, 1994, 146-57.

------ (1807) *Corinne ou l'Italie*, Paris: Garnier Frères, n.d; trans. trans. Avriel Goldberger as *Corinne or Italy*, New Brunswick, NJ.: Rutgers, 1987.

------ (1814a) 'An Appeal to the Sovereigns Convened in Paris to Grant the Abolition of the Slave Trade', trans. Sharon Bell in Doris Kadish and Françoise Massardier-Kenney (eds) *Translating Slavery: Gender & Race in French Women's Writing, 1783-1823*, Kent, Ohio: Kent State University Press, 1994, 157-59.

------ (1814b) 'Preface to the Translation of a Work by Mr. Wilberforce on the Slave Trade', trans. Sharon Bell in Doris Kadish and Françoise Massardier-Kenney (eds) *Translating Slavery: Gender & Race in French Women's Writing, 1783-1823*, Kent, Ohio: Kent State University Press, 1994, 159-62.

------ (1816) 'The Spirit of Translations', trans. Doris Kadish in Doris Kadish and Françoise Massardier-Kenney (eds) *Translating Slavery: Gender & Race in French Women's Writing, 1783-1823*, Kent, Ohio: Kent State University Press, 1994, 162-67.

The volume 'Translating Slavery', edited by Doris Kadish and Françoise Massardier-Kenney, includes translations of Madame de Staël, Olympe de Gouges and Claire de Duras, women contemporaries who attacked slavery. The translations frankly downplay any inadvertent offensiveness of Madame de Staël. The excellent critical material in the volume makes the translators' work sound biased. It is not. It is simply that when confronted with a lexical choice that could make their author sound patronizing or colonial, they have chosen the least offensive alternative.

Stendhal (Henri Beyle) (1838-1840) *La Chartreuse de Parme*, edited by Béatrice Didier, Paris: Gallimard Folio Classique, 1972; trans. C. K. Scott Moncrieff as *The Charterhouse of Parma*, New York: Liveright, 1925.

Straight, H. Stephen (ed) (1994) *Languages Across the Curriculum* (Translation Perspectives 7), Binghamton: State University of New York at Binghamton. Out of print.

------ (1997) *Languages Across the Curriculum II* (Translation Perspectives 10): Binghamton: State University of New York at Binghamton.

Villiers de l'Isle-Adam (1885) *L'Eve future*, Paris: Jean-Jacques Pauvert, 1960; trans. Marilyn Gaddis Rose as *Eve of the Future Eden*, Lawrence, Kansas: Coronado Press, 1981; trans. Robert M. Adams as *Tomorrow's Eve*, Urbana: University of Illinois, 1982, out of print.

------ (1890) *Axël*, edited by Pierre Mariel, Paris: La Colombe, 1960; trans. H. P. R. Finberg, London: Jarolds, 1925; trans. Marilyn Gaddis Rose, Dublin: 1970; Reprinted London: Soho, 1985.

Yeats, W. B. (1938) *A Vision*, New York: Macmillan, 1956.

------ (1971) *Variorum Edition of the Poetry*, edited by Peter Allt and Russell K. Alspach, New York: Macmillan.

Critical Texts Cited. These works are noted either in the body of the foregoing monograph, its footnotes or its glossary. Although listed alphabetically, they were determined partly by the works I chose for my illustrations, partly by my approach.

Banner, Angelika (ed) (1994) *Displacements. Identities in Question*, Bloomington: Indiana University Press.

Benjamin, Walter (1916) 'On the Language of Men and Language as Such', in *Reflections*, trans. Edmund Jephcott, New York: Schocken, 1978.

------ (1923) 'The Task of the Translator', in *Illuminations*, trans. Harry Zohn, New York: Schocken Books, 1969.

These brief, aphoristic essays should be read early in one's entry into comparative literature and translation studies. As a matter of fact, knowledge of them is usually assumed. They profit from stereoscopic reading. Indeed, these two gallant translators have been criticized for normalizing syntax. However, for native English speakers, it is probably wise to start with Zohn and Jephcott and then go back to Benjamin to see where the interliminal space has been curtailed. (The French translation by philosopher Maurice Gondillac has been criticized for over-interpretive inaccuracies. However, Derrida in the 'Babel' essay listed below used this French translation, not the German original.) The 'Gesammelte Schriften' are published by Suhrkamp Verlag (Frankfurt-am-Main, 1972).

Bhabha, Homi K. (1994) *The Locale of Culture*, New York: Routledge.

Block, Haskell M. (1977) 'Poe, Baudelaire and His Rival Translators', in Marilyn Gaddis Rose (ed) *Translation in the Humanities*, Binghamton: State University of New York at Binghamton, 59-66.

------ (1984) 'Poe, Baudelaire and the Problem of the Untranslatable', *Translation Perspectives* 1: 104-112.

Brisset, Annie (1990) *Sociocritique de la traduction: Théâtre et altérité au Québec (1968-1988)*, Longueuil, Québec: Le Préambule.

Brower, Reuben (1974) *Mirror on Mirror*, Cambridge, Mass.: Harvard University Press. *An elegantly diachronic discussion that shows how translations from Classical Greek and Latin reflect the prevailing high culture of an era.*

Budick, Sanford and Wolfgang Iser (eds) (1996) *The Translatability of Cul-*

ture. Figurations of the Space Between, Palo Alto: Stanford University. *These symposia proceedings are uneven, but Klaus Reichert's analysis of the Buber-Rosenzweig Bible translation uses the notion of space the way 'interliminal' is used in the foregoing monograph.*

Caws, Mary Ann (1983) 'Insertion in an Oval Frame: Poe Circumscribed by Baudelaire', in Harold Bloom (ed) *Charles Baudelaire*, New York: Chelsea House, 1987, 101-124. *Caws points to echoes and images of the Poe tale in a Baudelaire poem sequence. She concludes by pointing out that Baudelaire's translation of the tale was in itself a framing.*

Collier, Peter (1990) *Literary Theory Today*, Ithaca: Cornell University.

Derrida, Jacques (1980) 'Des Tours de Babel', in Joseph Graham (ed) *Difference in Translation*, Ithaca, NY: Cornell University, 1985, 209-248. *This is Derrida's own reading of Benjamin's essay and was originally conceived as an answer to Steiner's 'After Babel'. All Derrida's translators have followed neoliteralism before the fact and hav probably influenced translating for American academic presses.*

------ (1987) 'Geschlecht, II: Heidegger's Hand', trans. John P. Leavey Jr., in John Sallis (ed) *Deconstruction and Philosophy*, Chicago: University of Chicago.

------ (1991) *Donner le temps*, Paris: Galilée; trans. Peggy Kamuf as *The Gift of Time*, Chicago: University of Chicago, 1992.

Dingwaney, Anuradha and Carol Maier (eds) (1995) *Between Languages and Cultures. Translation and Cross-Cultural Texts*, Pittsburgh: University of Pittsburgh. *The emphasis here is on Western translations modifying non-Western work to make it marketable and, it is charged, ideologically acceptable. However, Maier's introduction 'Towards a Theoretical Practice for Cross-Cultural Translations' works toward a strategy of fairness.*

Faber, Pamela (1989) 'Charles Baudelaire and His Translation. Edgar Allen Poe', *Meta* 34: 253-58.

Farias, Victor (1989) *Heidegger and Nazism*, trans. Paul Burrell and Dominic Di Bernardi; Gabriel R. Ricci, Philadelphia: Temple University.

Gadamer, Hans-Georg (1960) *Truth and Method*, trans. Garrett Barden and John Cumming, New York. Seabury, 1975. *From Part 3 Gadamer uses translating as his metaphor for communication and makes many insightful comments about translation. The German publisher is J.C.B. Mohr (Tübingen, 1960).*

Heylen, Romy (1993) *Translation, Poetics, and the Stage*, New York: Routledge. *A polysystem approach to Hamlet in translation.*

Larson, Mildred (1984) *Meaning-based Translation. A Guide to Cross-Language Equivalence*, Lanham, MD.: University Press of America. *A no-nonsense guide to translation practice by a longtime administrator and supervisor of the Wycliffe Bible Translators (Summer Institute of Linguistics). Its examples are generally from non-Western languages.*

Lefevere, André (1981) 'Beyond the Process: Literary Translation and Translation Theory', in Marilyn Gaddis Rose (ed) *Translation Spectrum*, Albany: SUNY Press, 52-59. *This fairly early succinct and non-polemical explanation of the polysystem perspective presents as much of the strategy as a literary translator or teacher of literature in translation will need. With a few well-chosen examples Lefevere shows how translations can be used to introduce innovations that will change literary norms.*

Levinas, Emmanuel (1974) *L'Autrement qu'être ou au-delà de l'essence*, The Hague: Martinus Nijoff.

------ (1981) *Otherwise than Being*, trans. Alphonso Lingis, The Hague: Martinus Nijhoff. *Levinas's message that communication occurs despite insurmountable non-simultaneity that lets in change (and the risk of non-communication) is inscribed in his rhapsodic style, painstakingly rendered by Lingis. See my 'Levinas and Translation Theory' below.*

Lyotard, Jean-François (1983) *Le Différand*, Paris: Editions de Minuit.

------ (1988) *The Differand. Phrases in Dispute*, trans. George Van Den Abbeele, St. Paul: University of Minnesota. *Lyotard's concept of the 'différand' is akin to aporia and gap, 'différance' and 'manque' in French, and 'Abstand' in German. All are attempts to name what lies between a word and its referent(s). See my 'Translation and 'Le Différand''below.*

Mallarmé, Stéphane (1886) 'Avant-dire au Traité du verbe par René Ghil', *Œuvres complètes*, edited by Henri Mondor and G. Jean-Aubry, Paris: Gallimard Pléiade, 1945, 857- 58.

Mounin, Georges (1976) *Linguistique et traduction*, Brussels: Dessart et Mardaga.

Nida, Eugene A. (1946/1975) *Language Structure and Translation. Essays*, edited by Anwar S. Dill, Palo Alto: Stanford University.

------ and Charles Tabor (1974) *Theory and Practice of Translation*, Leiden: E.J. Brill.

------ and Jan de Waard (1986) *From One Language to Another*, Nashville, TN: Thomas Nelson.

Any essay by Nida is relevant and timely because he himself has kept with the vanguard he helped form. A beginning researcher could profitably begin study with selections from the Dill anthology. Although a sociolinguist, Nida is sympathetic and conversant with the perspectives that have failed to supercede his. For many years an executive with the American Bible Society, Nida is quietly but unabashedly Protestant; for this reason his books with Tabor and de Waard, which use examples from the Christian New Testament, will not be so helpful to students generally as those in the Dill anthology.

Richardson, Joanna (1994) *Baudelaire*, New York: St. Martin's.

Robinson, Douglas (1991) *The Translator's Turn*, Baltimore: Johns Hopkins.

------ (1996) *Translation and Taboo*, DeKalb, IL: Northern Illinois Press.

Robinson is quite possibly the most original theorist writing today. He refuses summarizing. He will not settle into a position and stay put. But from each position he takes, he finds a new, illuminating angle for discussing translation. He also manifests an infectious glee with language. Beginning researchers may want to postpone these works until they have read the knowledge Robinson assumes, such as Benjamin, Nida above, Steiner and Venuti below. In 'The Translator's Turn' Robinson takes up two experiences of translating: somatics (what feels right) and dialogics (mediating between the author and the probable reader).

Rose, Marilyn Gaddis (1970) 'Milton, Chateaubriand, and Villiers de L'Isle-Adam: *Paradise Lost* and *Axël*', *Studies in Romanticism* 9: 37-43.
This takes up Chateaubriand's mediation as translator and promoter of Milton.

------ (1984) 'Source Sovereignty and Target Taste', in Will L. McLendon (ed) *L'Hénaurme Siècle*, Heidelberg: Carl Winter, 217-30. *This is a descriptive translation study featuring De Staël's 'Corinne' in English.*

------ (1990) 'Translation and *Le Différand*. The relation of Lyotard's epistemology to translation', *Meta* 35: 126-32.

------ (1995) '*Angoisse, Jouissance*, and *Volupté*. Levinas and Translation Theory', in Peter W. Krawutschke (ed) *Connections*, Medford, New Jersey: Information Today, 381-88. *This presentation 'translates' via paraphrase Levinas's discourse on language into standard exposition and from thence applies it to translating. That is, once a saying (Dire) becomes a said (Dit) in one language, it can become a said (Dit) in another language with a heightening of non-simultaneity, a lessening of correlation of the signifieds, and a greater possibility of saying otherwise in the said.*

------ (1996) 'Do Authors Control Translators. Second Thoughts by a translator of *L'Eve future*', in John Anzalone (ed) *Jeering Dreamers*, Amsterdam: Rodopi.

Steiner, George (1975) *After Babel*, New York: Oxford. *Time has changed the significance of this highly readable discussion of literature and literary translation. In the mid-1970s critics discussed Steiner's description of the translation process ('the hermaneutic motion') and his division of perspectives between Benjamin and American linguist Noam Chomsky. (In retrospect it would seem that Chomsky's Universal Grammar could make room for Benjamin's pure language.) Now, nearly a quarter of a century later, we can be grateful to Steiner for bringing translation studies as a discipline to the attention of the educated public and for recuperating Benjamin's two essays.*

Toury, Gideon (1995) *Descriptive Translation Studies and Beyond*, Amsterdam: John Benjamins. *Along with his dissertation adviser Itamar Even-Zohar, Toury conceptualized the polysystem. Since the late 1970s he has stayed with it and refined it for this collection, which contains new versions of some of his first published analyses. Polysystem implies several literary systems within a single system, e.g. popular literature, children's literature, advertising and propaganda as well as serious literature. Toury believes that translations are particularly revelatory of the norms coming in and circulating in a system. His own country Israel, a new nation with successive waves of immigration, has given him a historical 'laboratory' for finding where former national languages like Russian, German and English have influenced Hebrew and Hebrew literature. It is very clarifying for beginning researchers. Aiming for objectivity, he tends to hypostatize concepts and entities so that ST and TT become capital letters in an algebra and not, say, Tom Sawyer in English and Hebrew. In this collection of essays the term 'polysystem' is used only in one footnote where he is quoting Even-Zohar.*

Wilson, Edmund (1931) *Axel's Castle*, New York: Charles Scribner's Sons.

Wilss, Wolfram (1985) 'The Role of the Translator in the Translation Process', *Translation Perspectives* 2: 13-14.

Part Two. Other Critical Texts Relevant for Literary Translation

These are works I find valuable but had no cause to cite directly in the preceding monograph. Please bear in mind that I find any conceptually challenging work bearing on language and culture potentially applicable to translating and to reading literature in translation stereoscopically.

Barnstone, Willis (1993) *The Poetics of Translation*, New Haven: Yale University Press. *A genial, wide-ranging poetry translator presents his own personal but rather Benjaminian amalgamation of history, theory and practice.*

Biguenet, John and Rainer Schulte (eds) (1989) *The Craft of Translation*, Chicago: University of Chicago Press. *This anthology makes accessible the credos of nine accomplished American literary translators (Gregory Rabassa, Margaret Sayers Peden, Burton Raffel, Edmund Keeley, Donald Frame, John Felstiner, William Weaver, Christopher Middleton and Edward Seidensticker). All conceptualize their experience and in so doing demonstrate that literary translating is intimately linked to the personal history of the translator. To me they demon-*

strate that calling a good translator one who is able to follow the norms denies the very real existence of genius.

Bly, Robert (1983) *The Eight Stages of Translation*, Boston: Rowan Tree. *A controversial American poet who brought Latin American poetry into the contemporary repertory explains how he reaches his final translation of a Rilke sonnet.*

Foucault, Michel (1966) *Les mots et les choses*, Paris: Gallimard.

------ (1970) *The Order of Things*, trans. anon., New York: Pantheon.

At the beginning of his career Foucault translated Kant, and his work as both a translator and a translated author lends itslf to stereoscopic reading. Despite the basically neoliteral strategy that his translators have increasingly taken, there are spaces between the boundaries of text and translation(s) that are literally meaningful. For example, since he establishes his own sexual orientation through his adroit choices of grammatical gender in nouns and active and passive modes of verbs, any reader without access to the French text misses the infrastructure. In my opinion, Foucauldian essays can illuminate literary criticism and from there be applied both to reading and translating, especially when we are dealing with eras where he has analyzed the dominant epistemology of the signs and referents. We could have used his revisionist medieval symbology in discussing Baudelaire or Villiers de l'Isle-Adam.

Honig, Edwin (1985) *The Poet's Other Voice*, Amherst: University of Massachusetts. *Interviews with Willard Trask, John Hollander, Herbert Mason, Ben Belitt, Richard Wilbur, Robert Fitzgerald, Max Hayward, Edmund Keeley, Octavio Paz, Michael Hamburger and Christopher Middleton.*

Lefevere, André (1975) *Translating Poetry. Seven Strategies and a Blueprint*, Assen: Van Gorcum. *This tour de force takes Catullus no. 64 through translations from 1870 to 1969 to show the options that are still current in English-language poetry.*

Levine, Suzanne Jill (1991) *The Subsversive Scribe*, St. Paul, MN: Grey Wolf. *Levine takes a reader through her re-creations of contemporary Latin American writing. Formidable literary analysis is not only a first step but an ongoing process along with the translating.*

Venuti, Lawrence (ed) (1992) *Rethinking Translation*, London: Routledge.

------ (1995) *The Translator's Invisibility*, London: Routledge.

The title essay in 'The Translator's Invisibility' should come early in beginner scholarly research, along with Nida and Benjamin – probably before Robinson, since Robinson assumes knowledge of these three. This essay, which first appeared in 1986, was the first to challenge both Nida's notion of dynamic equivalence and the hitherto accepted norm that a translation should not sound like one. Venuti gave us the terms 'foreignizing' (which I have renamed 'neoliteral') and 'domesticating'. His was a consciousness-raising about the ethics of colonizing appropriations in translation. (Nida has been a Bible translator, and this means he believes the Bible is needed by those who do not have access to it, in other words, translation to strengthen Western hegemony.) 'Rethinking Translation' is an anthology in which essayists expose the fallacy of ideologically neutral translation, especially for Francophone writers of Egypt, the Maghreb and Quebec.

General Introductions

The following books were planned to guide beginning graduate students with regard to where the field was heading.

Rose, Marilyn Gaddis (ed) (1996) *Translation Horizons. Beyond the Boundaries of 'Translation Spectrum'* (Translation Perspectives 9), Binghamton: State University of New York at Binghamton. *Eclectic by design, this anthology represents both empirical and speculative translation studies, including essays by Eugene Nida, Douglas Robinson and Lawrence Venuti. Literary criticism is highlighted by most essayists (such as Carrol Coates, André Lefevere, Carol Maier, Françoise Massardier-Kenney, Gregory Rabassa and the editor.)*

------ (ed) (1981) *Translation Spectrum*, Albany: State University of New York Press. *Although this textbook is superseded by the preceding volume, there are no duplications. The theoretical pieces have dated somewhat, but the period and genre essays are still valid, dealing with areas such as translating art songs, Arabic poetry, medieval drama, drama since Ibsen. Here also is found Lefevere's demonstration of how the polysystem works in literary criticism. See above.*

Neubert, Albrecht and Gregory Schreve (1992) *Translation as Text*, Kent, Ohio: Kent State University Press. *Neubert, a specialist in Anglo-American literature, and Shreve, a linguist, have collaborated to make translation studies more systematic. The book makes a strong appeal to graduate students because it conveys a very confident empiricism. Its categories and checklists aim at demystifying the translation process. Unlike 'Translation Horizons', to which both contributed, and which aims at laying out a spectrum, this monograph keeps its focus on empirical studies.*

Part III. Conspicuous Absences

Aside from *Translating Slavery* (Kadish and Massardier-Kenney 1994), there are no feminist works on this list. This is chiefly because I have always looked for the absent woman while I read.

Nor are there histories of translation studies to be found here. Those available are histories of translation in the West. The *Routledge Encyclopedia of Translation Studies* (1998) should rectify this situation, although readers will be obliged to compose the synopticon themselves.

TRANSLATION THEORIES EXPLAINED
Series Editor: Anthony Pym, Spain
ISSN 1365-0513

Other Titles in the Series

Translating as a Purposeful Activity, Christiane Nord
Translation and Gender, Luise von Flotow
Translation and Language, Peter Fawcett
Translation and Empire, Douglas Robinson
Conference Interpreting, Roderick Jones

Forthcoming in 1998

Contemporary Approaches to Translation Teaching, Donald Kiraly
Translation in Systems, Theo Hermans

Also Available from St. Jerome

Dictionary of Translation Studies, Mark Shuttleworth & Moira Cowie
Western Translation Theory from Herodotus to Nietzsche, Douglas
Robinson
Wordplay and Translation, edited by Dirk Delabastita
Traductio. Essays on Punning and Translation, edited by Dirk
Delabastita
Method in Translation History, Anthony Pym

Plus

The Translator. Studies in Intercultural Communication, a refereed
international journal edited by Mona Baker

Also Available through St. Jerome Publishing

Titles from the United States, India, Finland, Spain, France and Germany

Communication Across Cultures, Basil Hatim
The Medieval Translator 4, edited by Roger Ellis & Ruth Evans
Translation and Multilingualism. Postcolonial Contexts, edited by
    Shantha Ramakrishna
Recent Trends in Empirical Translation Research, edited by Sonja
    Tirkkonen-Condit and John Laffling
Topics in Interpreting Research, edited by Jorma Tommola
Translation & Knowledge, edited by Yves Gambier & Jorma Tommola
Language Transfer and Audiovisual Communication. A Bibligoraphy,
    Yves Gambier
Les Formations en traduction et interprétation, Monique Caminade &
    Anthony Pym
Translation and the Manipulation of Discourse, edited by Peter Jansen
Overcoming Language Barriers in Television, Georg-Michael Luyken et al.
Dubbing and Subtitling: Guidelines for Production & Distribution,
    Josephine Dries
Epistemological Problems in Translation and Its Teaching, Anthony Pym
Acculturation of the Other: Irish Milieux in Finnish Drama Translation,
    Sirkku Aaltonen

Translation Perspectives Series, published by the State University of New York at Binghamton General Editor: Professor Marilyn Gaddis Rose

Vol. I	*Selected Papers 1982-83*
Vol. II	*Selected Papers 1984-85*
Vol. III	*Selected Papers 1985-86*
Vol. IV	*Selected Papers 1986-87*
Vol. V	*Hermeneutics & the Poetic Motion*
Vol. VI	*Translating Latin America*
Vol. VIII	*Translation: Religion, Ideology, Politics*
Vol. IX	*Translation Horizons*
Vol. X	*Using Languages Across the Curriculum*

Of related interest

Critical Theory. Western and Indian, edited by Prafulla C. Kar
Literary Theory. (Re) Reading Culture and Aesthetics, edited by Jameela
   Begum & B. Hariharan
Post-Colonial African Fiction. The Crisis of Consciousness, Mala Pandurang
Postmodernism and Feminism. Canadian Contexts, edited by Shirin Kudchedkar

Translation Studies Abstracts

Published as one volume of two issues per year (approximately 192 pages, June and December).
ISSN 1460-3063. Available from St. Jerome Publishing

TSA is a new initiative designed to provide a major and unique research tool, primarily for scholars of translation and interpreting. It is the first abstracting service of its kind, focusing on and covering all aspects of research within the domain of translation studies, including translation theory, interpreting, history of translation, process-oriented studies, corpus-based studies, translation and gender, translation and cultural identity, translator training/pedagogy, translation policies, bible/religious translation, literary translation, screen translation, technical & legal translation, machine (-aided) translation, terminology, community/dialogue interpeting, conference interpreting, court interpreting, and signed language interpreting.

Translation studies has many points of contact with other disciplines, especially linguistics, pragmatics, comparative literature, cultural studies, gender studies, postcolonial studies, corpus linguistics, anthropology, ethnography, and any field of study concerned with the history of ideas. Scholars working in any of these fields will find much of direct relevance in *TSA*.

***TSA* Editor:** Sara Laviosa, UMIST & University of Birmingham, UK
Consulting Editors: Andrew Chesterman (Finland), Birgitta Englund Dimitrova (Sweden), Adolpho Gentile (Australia), Theo Hermans (UK), Rosa Rabádan (Spain), Ronald Sim (Kenya), Gideon Toury (Israel) and Maria Tymoczko (USA).

Subscription to Volume 1 (1998)
Institutional: £55/$89, plus postage & packing.
Individual: £25/$40, plus postage & packing.

Bibliography of Translation Studies (Companion to *TSA*)
ISBN 1-900650-13-4. Available free for subscribers to *TSA*. Price for non-subscribers: £9/$15, plus postage & packing.